W9-AQQ-435

# Jane's Stories
## An Anthology of Work by Midwestern Women

Edited by
Glenda Bailey-Mershon
Clara Johnson
Linda Mowry
Julie Sass

Wild Dove Studio and Press, Inc.
Palatine, Illinois

PUBLISHED BY
Wild Dove Studio and Press, Inc.
P.O. Box 789
Palatine, Illinois 60078-0789

This edition copyright © 1994 by Wild Dove Studio and Press, Inc.

All rights reserved. No part of the contents of this book may be reproduced or transmitted in any form or by any means without the written permission of the publisher. Reprint rights may be sought from the individual authors and artists whose work is published herein. Reproduction for educational purposes only may be granted by the publisher.

Jane's Stories: An Anthology of Work by Midwestern Women/ Edited by Glenda Bailey-Mershon, Clara Johnson, Linda Mowry, and Julie Sass.

ISBN 0-9639894-0-5

Printed and bound in the United States of America.

# CONTENTS

# Acknowledgements and Dedication

The editors wish to acknowledge the group of women called *Jane* who founded and operated an underground abortion providers' network in the days before Roe v. Wade. Their courage and commitment are a symbol of Midwestern feminism and served as inspiration for this book.

Wild Dove Studio and Press, Inc. wishes to acknowledge the feminist community of the Northwest suburbs, particularly Northwest Suburban NOW and the cooperative owners of Prairie Moon, Ltd., Feminist Bookstore, all of whom have nurtured this project.

*Jane's Stories* is dedicated to all those women who take risks for their sisters.

## Cinda Thompson

### Alive and Writing and From the Midwest

My grandmother took her granddaughters to a graveyard deep in the country each Memorial Day and sat beneath the spreading limbs of a sycamore. She crocheted as she recited the names of carpenters, circuit riders, seamstresses, homemakers, school teachers, bandits, and bankers. She knew the name of the Native American who once walked among us, the names of our mothers, fathers, grandparents — relatives, ancestors all — and we children laughed among the grave sites. We darted in and out among the woods surrounding them. We played hide-and-seek between both the tree trunks and the tombstones and were not afraid. The veined leaves overhead played patterns of dark and light across the green grass, across every warm and deepening evening.

Trees rooted within the hills and flatlands alike. Trees, standing solitary or planted in stands between the fields of farmland. Trees growing on the shores of both mirrored lakes and rivers as muddy as the Mississippi. Trees pouring over the countryside, over each and every out-of-town roadside. Trees say the most about being home in the Midwest.

A maple tree shaded our house on West Main Street, Smalltown, U.S.A. A willow tree was desired by my mother and so planted by my father along the back boundary of our yard. The lofty maple shaded my bedroom, but its height made a climb out of the question. The eldest of three daughters, I finally managed to gather the courage of my younger sisters and climb to a fork in the willow. The feeling of trees all around had begun long before sojourns spent in the willow, however.

The trees that lined the lake on which my grandparents stayed in their cabin seemed older, for instance. We girls went swinging on an old tire hung from a great, tall oak, went swinging out over the lake. We spotted frogs. We called after the catfish below the surface, after the bluegill. I can still see myself as a girl child, still feel my young body stretch and soar out over the water.

We sisters took note of the uncles or cousins gathered below us — who smoked and who drank, who didn't. We knew which aunt wore what shade of lipstick or what scent of "new-fangled" perfume, which relation spoke of being most recently moved by "the Holy Spirit." Most of all, we children noted who came to play, who came to lift our bodies up over his or her head, to swing us high enough to reach for the trees....

We were an extended family system over which my grandmother and grandfather seemed to reign. My grandfather had worked in a big job all the way out in Washington, D.C. When he retired, he wore fishing caps laden with gaudy hooks and flies, and plaid flannel shirts, soft against my cheek. My grandmother, her hands covered in flour or cornmeal, fried "a mess of fish" under the trees on so many summer nights of all our lives. And she could roll out pie dough in "nothing flat." Both grandparents could remember "way back."

We sisters dropped our lines into the water. We grew up in between my grandparents, as did the fathers, mothers, children all around us. My grandparents, who stood like trees themselves — old, gnarled, but forever firm in memory.


The almost-teenaged girl I can see now, so much more clearly than before, climbed the willow tree back in town and did not think too much on all that had come before her. Secretly, she had begun to worry not that so much noise, but so much silence passed between her parents. However, in those middle-class 1950's days in which she was growing taller, this eldest girl desired silence. She wanted to escape the screaming of the younger children across the back lawn, the eyes of her ever-watchful father who sat in the swing and read the paper, the more pointed vigilance of her mother, whose face appeared now and then through the kitchen window as she did the supper dishes, as she watched the clock and counted minutes until bathtime and bedtime.

Growing toward adolescence, the girl climbed toward the silver underside of narrow, weeping leaves, wanting to look beyond the house of her parents.

She straddled the limb of the tree and could see Main Street. She wondered at the old couple from the country who planted corn in their backyard right next door. They bent and rose together. Not the way her parents worked in town, she knew.

The girl's eyes followed Main Street downtown toward "the Square" and the county courthouse, the red brick library, home of the Bobbsy Twins and Nancy Drew. Already in the back of the child's mind were the questions: What really went on in that courthouse? What did a mayor do, exactly? As a matter of fact, what did "government" do? Her father and his friends discussed politics in the yard at night. They stood in groups and talked underneath her bare legs, which the turning-of-age young lady had already decided to ask her mother if she could shave.

The girl already knew of the trees that grew beyond the Square, over beyond the tracks. She had been down there on Sunday afternoons when she had ridden with her father to get a block of ice for a picnic. From her spot in the willow, the girl viewed those roads only barely familiar — narrow roads, some completely covered by the branches of stooping trees, trees that seemed to grow wild, trees whose tops bent completely over these particular streets because there was not enough city money to prune the trees of "those people."

The girl had heard the stories of the neighbors. One of the women who came to sit in the yard talked of seeing, in her childhood, an African-American man in trouble, a man beaten and tied with a rope and then dragged behind a wagon. Who knew what the branches overhead held for him? The neighbor who'd once been a child had said she'd cried at the sight. Cried out of fright and for another's suffering. Cried that such violence existed, and that it seemed to exist never-ending in this, her homeland.

The young girl in the tree squinted her eyes and wondered at the existence of strangers. Strangers who had whole lives, whole parts in the town, whole histories not her own, roots that went from this land back into another land. Eventually she learned of other groups as well — and that all those people around her were just some assortment of groups, really. The African, the Irish, German, English, Scottish, Welsh, the Italian, the Eastern European, all who came to clear the woods, settle the farmlands, live in tents beside the mines in a desperate scramble for survival. The Native American of her grandmother's line who had all but disappeared, although the girl's parents had taken her to see the displays in a museum once.

The branches of the willow spread out around the young girl. Spring green branches growing thicker, heavier, sweeping the ground, evidently never quite clean.

She had not learned until high school that the land beneath her feet had long since been stained. Stained by wars with the Blackhawk, the Iroquois, "problems" with the Cherokee, part of her own family tree. And there had been the Civil War: those enslaved who had dashed for freedom, those hidden and those returned into bondage. A war in which not only states went their own way, but counties and towns had also tried to secede. Brothers, sisters, every separate limb of a family had gone this way and that. And there had been religious wars. The Mormons driven out. And the Klan. And the frenzied activities of bootleggers in the night-time glades.

Many an old-timer in overalls who sat on the Square spitting tobacco had talked of being sent "all the way off to Europe" to fight in 1917. The girl pressed for stories from her own father, stories of tea in England in World War II, the Air Force, bombings in London, France, Germany. Did her father know about the Holocaust?

A girlfriend's father had served in Korea. And then Vietnam. Even in the Midwest, the tree-lined streets were suddenly filled with students and the National Guard all around. The young woman sat in a tree above a college campus and read "American Classics" for literature class, at the same time listening to both sides down in the street: the soldier back from Vietnam and the dissenter alike who spoke of a brother in the army, the lottery, a fiancee about to be drafted. They spoke of a country called Cambodia. Of one called Laos.

Straws can be driven like spears into trees by the tornadoes that rip through the Midwest: violent, often misinterpreted, even misunderstood ill winds. Rarely are these straws, these bits of twig removed. Rather, they become the subject of wonder and discussion, by some who remember the tree without the stiff shaft driven through its very center, by others because — "Look! Would you just look at this thing now become a part of the tree!"

The trees with which people in the Midwest are most comfortable grow twisted, not straight. And the natives have a habit of attributing wisdom to older trees. Wisdom is somehow related to endurance, meaning that these trees have lasted. And everyone knows that new nests have a better chance of being hidden between the lacy branches of a tree that has withstood lightening and thunder, storms and fire.

The rings of an old tree grow around and around and around its center, the trunk and the branches growing up and around each knothole. The limbs offer dark shade and solace for that pain for which there is no solace. There is war and more war. The trees simply wait and shake their lofty heads in the breeze.

The girl, finally grown into a woman, had a chance to escape further than the fork of her parents' willow tree. She had an opportunity to leave the Midwest, to go further than those horizons that stretched out around her. She'd finally decided to become a writer, and writers — she'd gotten the impression in her literature classes — should see the world. Artists must "experience."

But then what to write? She had been disillusioned with the life of her "ideal" family, the narrow limitations of a mostly-white and middle-class hometown and its prejudices. Indeed, she saw the narrowness, the prejudice of not only home, but of whole regions, whole states. But as she grew older, there was also the disillusion with the lives of "the wild," the rich, the famous, and the none-too-romantic, with the lure of alcohol and the "absence" so often present in the life of abandon.

Once, as a fellow traveler drove, I fell asleep in the back of a van and then woke up suddenly in the middle of green. In the middle of trees. I was a girl again, and I was home.

But the pen and what to write? All those familiar voices that come whispering across water and across ashes. Across a lake called childhood and the call of the bobwhite, a past comes murmuring up.

A tree weeps the lullaby of men who forever return to the inland woods to fish. Intricate branches whisper the name of a grandmother who crocheted patterns from underneath a sycamore. Of my great — or was it my great-great? — grandmother, who wove tribal patterns in some land of time beyond us all.

Woman, come home. Writer, a pen beckons — from the Midwest.

*Washington Island.* Ink with watercolor,
copyright © 1994 by Cherie B. Weil.

## Evelyn E. Shockley

### The Poet

One day
I saw a poem
written on
a blade
of
grass.
(Whitman would have
approved.)
Its author was
invisible,
the poem said.
She could be seen
only in her
poetry.
Her poems were
a public display
of her whole self:
wet, naked, cold
and
fierce, blazing, tall.
The grass poem
was the first I found.
One fall,
I noticed her script
on the underside of
a maple leaf,
a prayer for
the rain forests.
One poem, weeping for
the children of Somalia,
was engraved
on the tines of a fork
in the deli on Dearborn.

I almost stepped on
the words she'd inscribed
on the thirteenth step
down the stairs to
the 95th Street
El stop:
she was looking for
a friend,
someone who wouldn't mind
massaging her scalp
from time to time.

\*    \*    \*    \*    \*

The poet became known
to me.
I heard her;
I saw her.
I know how it hurts
to comb her hair
after waiting too long
for a touch-up
she couldn't afford.
I know why her womb
remains unfilled.
I know when she
was called a black whore,
because she couldn't get
the doctor's hand
off her breast
fast enough to suit
her
or his wife.
I know where she keeps
a pint of Scotch.

\*    \*    \*    \*    \*

The last poem I found,
scribbled on a girl-child's
barrette,
testified to the sun:
its silence,
its futile routine,
its destructiveness,
its self-destructiveness.

The sun,
wrote the poet,
is still
powerful,
nurturing,
life-giving.
I am like the sun,
she insisted,
and I will kiss
its fiery face
and write my next poem
there!

## Connection

I was walking on South Stony Island when I saw you:
a Ghanaian princess, thinly disguised.
I stopped short and stared as you strode by,
just to be sure, and I was not mistaken.
You were not tall, but your back was straight
and your eyes boasted the viewpoint of a giant,
claimed to have seen everything and dismissed much of it.
Your dark hair was braided close to your head
and the ends were twisted up into a crown.
Gold pieces weighted your ears and embraced your fingers,
one hundred bracelets coiled around your arm
            from wrist to elbow,
and gold ropes were borne up by your breasts.
The bright orange fabric of your dress
stretched and clung to your roundnesses;
it announced your body without shame or invitation.
You stepped, without effort,
without changing the rhythm of your hips,
over and between the flattened beer cans,
the shards of glass, the empty Big Mac wrappers.
You looked neither to the right nor the left;
            you took it all in.
You gathered your people with a smiling flash of teeth;
you distanced them with a raised eyebrow or chin.
The reds, pinks, and bronzes brushed
across your lips, nails, and cheeks
were also woven deep within your mahogany skin.
Could I be the only one who recognized you?

## Woman to Woman

I guess it must have been at the end of my first year of high school when I realized that all of my friends were guys. Well, not all of them; I still had the two or three close girlfriends I had known since first grade. And I'd started hanging out with one of the "cool" girls in my class — I was definitely not a cool girl at the time, so it was an opportunity I couldn't resist.

But it seemed that ninety percent of the new friends I'd made by the end of that year were male. And this trend continued throughout high school. "Boys" — that's what they were then — were my confidants. They called me and we talked for hours. I teased them, made them behave, and demanded that they either <u>show</u> me a 1957 Mustang convertible or shut up talking about it. They let me in on the secrets of what they wanted from a girl — sometimes very wistful hopes, sometimes desires too horrible for my young heart to hear.

My mother cut her eyes and pursed her lips every time she answered the phone to hear one of them asking to speak with me. "Boys, boys, boys! That's all that ever calls this house is boys! You're too boy-crazy for your own good, " she warned, handing me the phone.

She was right, as she always is. I was hopelessly, irrevocably crazy about boys. Something about them was fascinating to me — call it the "masculine mystique." I wanted to hear more, more, about these very important cars, and their "horses" and their "top ends;" more about why Eddie Van Halen was the greatest living rock guitarist; more about how one of their friends — never they themselves — had run a complete game on two girls at different high schools. The stories about the scams never seemed to me to say anything bad about the boys, but rather made me disdain and pity the stupid girls who fell for these obvious tricks.

In college I positioned myself as "the girl who can hang with the guys." I dated no one, but had more male callers and ready escorts than the prettiest or easiest girls on campus. I was never at home alone on the weekends unless I wanted to be, even during prime dating hours. After all, when you run with a crew of twenty-odd guys, at least three or four of them at any given time will be pissed off at their girlfriend, abandoned to a girls' night out, or just plain unattached. Even when you take into account guys who were dating two or three women, they didn't spend every night of every weekend having sex.

The one who came closest to this possibility was Andre Ross. He could have any woman he wanted, any time he wanted. It was that simple. Although he was tall, had the clearest caramel skin, and beauty pageant teeth, it wasn't simply his looks. You can have all the sex appeal in the world, and some women still won't touch you when they know you're dating someone else. Andre was a master of the scam. He had the game down to an artistic science. A woman around Andre was only as safe as she was ugly.

He kept me in stitches over the lies he told, that women believed. After seven years of hearing the war stories of my friends, I, of course, was familiar with the subtlest falsehood; but I was convinced that only an idiot could fall for the lines he succeeded with. Then, too, I not only knew all the lines, but I also knew Andre. His "rep" was his life. He <u>had</u> to be known as the master. "Houdini" was the name he pledged under, and his motto was "I can get into places others only dream about."

Andre, Chris Horne, and a couple of the other better players usually came by my room after their escapades, to fill me in on the latest. One night, around 3:30 a.m., Andre knocked on my door. "Kelley! Kelleeeey! Open this muthfauckin' door, girl," he yelled, banging louder.

"Jesus! Come in!" I shouted back, as I opened the door to my cubbyhole. He was completely drunk. "Rum and coke?" I guessed, flipping on the lights.

"Jack Black." He sank to the floor. "I got that ass, though."

"Whose ass?" I climbed over him into my bed and pulled the covers up to my chest.

"Lauren's."

"No way! No fuckin' way!" I sat up. His inebriated grin answered me. "You did it! What happened?"

Andre had been trying for weeks — a long time, for him — to get in Lauren Harte's pants. She arrived on campus at the beginning of the year with a boyfriend "back home," and she had remained steadfastly faithful for almost the whole year. No one on campus could get <u>any</u> play. Inevitably, Chris challenged Andre to be the man.

Knowing that all of the amateur approaches had been tried, Andre took his time and watched and waited for that weak moment, and BOOM! He nailed her. I listened past this summary to some of the gory details, but the hour finally overcame me. "Dre, it's four a.m. Fucking go home and go to sleep."

"Kelley. Just let me sleep on your floor."

Andre, your room is just down two flights of stairs! I think you can make it. And turn out the light on your way out."

"Kelley, I'm going to sleep with Jack on your floor, or I'm going to earl on your floor."

"Fine. Sleep on the floor. Goodnight." I reached under the bed for one of my Nikes and threw it at the light switch. The first one missed, but the second one brought on darkness and sleep. The only other thing I remembered before noon the next day was Andre's loud-ass good-bye as he left sometime that morning.

I spent the rest of that Saturday holed up in the library, trying to get a paper out of the way before finals season. I closed the place down, and when I got back to my dorm room, I was too exhausted to listen to my messages and return calls. I crawled into bed. Outside, I could hear the faint sound of the bass driving the party going on in the lounge of the dorm across the street. It put me right to sleep.

Again, I was awakened by a knock on the door.

"Kelley?" The voice was female, so I knew I wasn't interested, especially at three a.m. But the knocking continued without letting up.

I finally crawled out of my bed, more than a little pissed, and went to the door. "Who is it?"

"Mara and Lauren." With my eyes wide, I let them in. I barely knew either Lauren or her best friend. I could only imagine that the visit had some connection to Andre's news.

"What can I do for you at three a.m.?"

"You can tell us what's up with your friend Andre," said Mara.

"Mara, I appreciate your coming with me, but I think I should speak with Kelley alone." She squeezed Mara's hands and gently closed my door behind her. Then she turned to me.

I couldn't anticipate what she was going to say and it was driving me crazy. If Andre wasn't through with her, I didn't want to say anything that would prevent him from going back.

"Kelley, let's be honest with each other about this," she began. We sat down on my bed.

"I don't know anything about it, " I warned her.

"Yes, you do. But let me ask you first: Did you know that Andre had a bet with Chris that he could sleep with 'the most impossible-to-fuck woman on campus'?"

I looked at her, seeing how much she wanted to hear me say no, but something stopped me from lying for Andre this time. "Yes."

Startled, she said, "You knew?"

"Yes. They told me weeks ago."

Lauren looked puzzled. "Well...well, what's up? Did he win?" I didn't get it. "I mean, I know it's personal and all, but it's important for me to know. You see, he has been wearing me down for a couple of months now, trying to get me to break up with Joel. He told me he loved me more than I could possibly imagine and we should be together. Frankly, it's very tempting. But I know his reputation, and I'm not crazy. I said, 'Prove it. Go without sex for four weeks, and I'll consider whether we can be together.'

"Well, the four weeks is up tomorrow and I have to make a decision. I don't want to make a mistake. Until today, I hadn't heard anything to make me think he had been with another woman. So I need to know — did you sleep with Andre last night?" I must have looked as confused as I felt, because she went on. "I mean, half the dorm heard him come into your room last night, and he didn't leave until this morning."

I almost laughed. "Oh, God. He <u>slept</u> here last night, but on the floor, passed out drunk. Why the hell would you assume we slept together?"

"He said so. Kelley, Mara heard him tell Chris and some other people that he won the bet last night around four a.m."

I was the most impossible-to-fuck woman on campus. I was impossible. I was to fuck. I was a woman.

I think my crying surprised me more than it did her. After a few moments face down in my pillow, I sat up and thanked her.

"For what?!"

I just smiled. "Girlfriend! Can we talk? Let me tell you what I know about Andre Ross."

## Bonnie Tunick

Monica Mary swallowed hard on the way to the principal's office. Clutching her rosary beads and mumbling a few quick Hail Marys, she knew she was in for it this time. Never to squirm out of a dare, she had snuck into the courtyard during study hall and hooked one of her mother's tattered brassieres onto a bust of old Mother Superior. Monica Mary was prepared to do the penance of her short lifetime.

**Stephanie Harris**

## Grounded

My socks were always falling down
and the emeralds and rubies on my fingers

came from a bubble-gum machine
but I wrote pages and pages of stories.

In one of them I was a witch —
I soared above the white-domed school

on my broomstick, sprinkling curses
like sugar.

Everyone looked up at me,
even the teacher.

They shouted up to me
but I wouldn't come down.

Then the wind blew my dress too high
and everyone started laughing.

When I landed in the playground,
they took away my broomstick.

The teacher made me sit up straight and
fold my hands, as though in prayer.

Everyone chanted around me...
I thought any minute I would go up in flames!

I ran home with my broomstick,
where I threw it in the back of the closet.

Now, years later,  my broomstick is broken
and I am stuck like a grounded bird.

Feminists have the best earrings:

hoops in the shape of fish eating their tails
wooden parrots painted shocking green

silver water-nymphs embracing amethyst crystals
rubber salamanders with red rhinestone eyes

women with short hair wear long earrings
sometimes two or three to one lobe

some wear cuffs in the shape of nude women,
small mountain-climbers straddling the outer rim

earrings have a language of their own
but you must lean in close to listen

decipher their murmured endearments
jingling like wind-chimes

as they caress the side of the neck
like strands of hair

and move when we move, and
catch the light and throw it back

we wear small discreet posts at funerals
so as not to offend the Angel of Death

and at job interviews and board meetings,
those faux pearl clips that pinch,

leaving small indentations, which throb for hours
while we're longing to wear wild animal shapes

and do a naked dance around a fire
until our senses swim and our fingers shoot sparks

the elder tribeswomen pass on their sacred earrings
to the next generation, with a story about each pair

where it came from, what its powers are
and the danger of being without earrings

when the enemy comes to call
so when you see a woman wearing black onyx
panthers

with emeralds for eyes, don't cross her path
the cats may be enchanted and the woman an
enchantress

anything can happen
when a woman wears earrings

## C. L. Fitzgerald

### An Indian on the El

I am unable to sleep tonight, thinking of the earth.
Indians too often do not reveal our feelings, especially
our pain.

I keep wondering what it was like before
we pursued Ph.D.'s;
worked for corporations; went out for cappuccino;
lived in urban areas; and rode electronic cars
through the sky.
How do Indians live in cities?
How do we touch the earth, revere her,
and have a relationship with her
when cities seem to have so little earth?

Pow wows are held in school gyms, and other places
with waxed wooden or cold concrete floors.
Our rhythm was made for dancing on the earth.
Pow wows are capitalistic and tourist events —
pay $5.00 at the gate — come and be entertained by
"real Indians;" learn all 'bout "real" Indians;
see "real" Indians.

I contemplate this unnatural life
in this man-made sphere called a "city."
I reflect upon this thought as I ride the El.
We glide, snake-like, by house tops, tennis courts, a YMCA,
graffitied buildings, high-rise structures
which touch the sky.
I think of my grandmother's garden
and the grape vineyards,
the apricot trees, and the mean-spirited blue jays
who chased the robins and all the other birds away.

When I close my eyes on the El, I see my mother
making and preparing the salmon for cooking.
I see my older sister brushing her waist-length hair.
She holds the whole of it by the bottom with the brush, then
releases it.
It fans out behind her like the wings of a bird,
black as a raven.

The El is full of people of all kinds.
They are not members of bands or clans.
Occasionally another Indian, looking less displaced than me,
boards the train. I wonder to which nation he belongs —
Apache, Seneca, Lakota?
I try to guess. It is a game I play with myself.

The El passes a billboard depicting running horses.
I wonder about my family's horses —
who is grooming them?
Do they miss the apples and carrots I used to bring?
Do they know I am living in a city and miss my weekends
with them?

I start to daydream about my "horse" weekends
with the wind in my hair,
and the smell of the horse is in my nostrils
as if I am actually there
riding on the horse's back.

I disembark at Wabash and Adams.
The thundering crowd carries me along
reminiscent of buffalo herds.
At work in the South Loop, I research and write grants
secretly dreaming of mountains, horses and wondering
about the growth of the white Iroquois corn this year.
I order Chinese food which is delivered to my office.
Through the office windows, the view is alleyways,
garbage dumpsters
and an array of homeless men standing about

with their hands in their pockets.
These men remind me of Indian men back on the res;
hoisting cans of beer from 24-packs at 9:00 a.m.
The scene is all too familiar.

The El returns me to my neighborhood after work.
The streets are a haven of people of all the sacred colors;
their diversity is the most natural feature of the city.
Like the natural world, they are rich with varying
colors, appearances, and scents.

Later, before I retire, I burn sage and pray,
an Iroquois prayer in Mohawk.
I am living in the city
but the city does not live in me.
I look out my living room window and see
an enormous moon
against a starless midnight blue sky.
I think: I am still an Indian.
It becomes a chant within my head:
I am still an Indian.
Riding on the El and living in a city
cannot change that.

Winter Vista
(dedicated to all Iroquois people—past, present, and future)

The land lies silent as the ice
on the bark of the white birch.
Overhead, a winter sky, gray as a river crane's egg,
its density curved into the thin crust
of frost covering the land.
Roads snake through hills and hollows.

We follow these roads down through hills
past birch-groves, through static villages
whose names are all that remain.
The land seems to whisper
in Onondaga, Seneca, Cayuga, Tuscarora,
Mohawk and Oneida.

In the Moon When the Snow Drifts
the frozen ground remembers feet;
snow-clad braves, raven hair
blowing fiercely in the winter's wind.
Earth has a long memory.
She recollects each child, bloody and warmed
by mothers' juices who has lived upon her ground.
She recalls straight rows of corn, bean, and squash;
the sturdy long-houses and sweatlodges
built upon her.
The crystalline lakes are flavored by the taste of men
who fished in their waters; of the women who split
the fish bellies open for the willow dryracks,
the dried fish smell piercing the crisp air.

We drive on, following the route
of warriors and ghosts.
Children wordless and remote,
wave at us from kindling porches.
We pass a frozen waterfall
held tightly in an icy fist.

Now the land levels for miles,
the white countryside unfolding before us
like yards of winding sheets.
Only the names of streets, lakes, and villages
are left to haunt our thoughts.
We have left behind the specters
whose white bones feed this phantom land.

## Judy Holman

### Riding into Reform

"It will be a delight to young girls to learn that their sex is, in itself, not a bar to riding the wheel."

Frances E. Willard

"A woman awheel is the picture of free, untrammeled womanhood."

Susan B. Anthony

Crossing the street the other morning, busy with personal thoughts, I almost stepped into the path of what I can only describe as a flying female projectile. Thankfully, I need not have worried about being hit. Seeing me long before I saw her, she eased around my body in one fluid move and left me standing in her breezy, perfumed wake. I watched her with the same soul-filling delight I've felt while watching hawks ride the wind. Her made-for-action, black and neon suit outlined her athletic body, which was working in harmony with her made-for-a-challenge bike. Looking neither right nor left, she flew straight-arrowed toward whatever personal goal she had set. I had no doubt that she would reach it, and, grinning, sent her a mental salute.

With a lighter step I resumed my walk, my thoughts turning naturally to another clear-eyed woman who, in 1892, saw the connection between women, bicycles and freedom. At age fifty-three, against the advice of friends and general public sentiment, she learned to ride. Experiencing the thrill, sense of mastery and health benefits first-hand, she wrote about them all in a little book called *How I Learned to Ride the Bicycle*. In 1895 it was a best seller. But, then, she was a far-sighted woman. Her name was Frances E. Willard.

Younger readers, so used to two-wheeled transportation, may be surprised to learn that women and bicycles were not an early or easy match. Much Victorian debris had to be swept off the cultural road before women were allowed their chance to ride. Debates raged about what it would do to women's health (read: reproductive organs), women's morals (read: a woman unchaperoned is a woman unchaste), and women's dress (read: remove the corset and it's a one-way ride to Cultural Decline.) It is no surprise that women like Frances Willard, already active in the Reform Movement, saw the bicycle as another vehicle for their emancipation.

From this we might assume that Frances Willard took to the wheel to Prove a Point. In fact, she learned to ride to improve her health. At fifty-three she suffered from "nerve-wear" and for good reason. For twenty years (1877-1897), she was President of the Women's Christian Temperance Union, the largest women's organization in the nineteenth century. Working in cooperative, parallel step with Susan B. Anthony and others, she focused her prodigious energy on the elimination of alcohol and the liquor trade. Alcoholism, a problem today, was disastrous for post-Victorian women still totally dependent on fathers and then husbands for survival. It was a massive task. At fifty-three, years of traveling, speaking, writing and organizing had taken its toll. Worn out, and mourning the death of her mother, Frances went to heal in the home of Lady Henry Somerset, her friend and President of the British W.C.T.U. It was there on that estate that Lady Somerset presented her with the bicycle she named "Gladys — that harbinger of health and happiness." Though a silent partner in this radical act, Gladys proved a patient teacher. Little by little, day by day, Frances found that, "She who succeeds in gaining the mastery of such an animal as Gladys will gain the mastery of life" (page 33).

*How I Learned to Ride the Bicycle* is the personal become political. Using her own experience with Gladys, Frances spoke to women about being focused on goals, the importance of will plus action, persistence in the face of defeat, and the necessity of appropriate mentors. She spoke to them about seeing success in order to experience it, keeping calm in the presence of fear, and how the freedom of movement was essential to their progress. In this case, freedom of movement meant freedom to come and go and freedom from tight, restrictive clothes.

Frances was particularly sensitive to this last issue, because, as she writes, "I ran wild until my sixteenth birthday, when the hampering long skirts were brought, with their accompanying corset and high heels; my hair was clubbed with pins....I remember the first heartbreak of a young human colt taken from its pasture..." (page 16). The bicycle, Frances knew, would necessitate a reform in clothing. Today, we read with sad humor her "radical" description of an appropriate riding outfit: "[A] skirt and blouse of tweed with belt, rolling collar and loose cravat, three inches from the ground; a round straw hat and walking shoes with gaiters...a simple modest suit to which no person of common sense could take exception" (page 75.) Tell that to the young woman in Spandex!

Women did learn to ride. Body-abusing corsets and sharp-eyed chaperones fell by the cultural way and Western civilization did not disintegrate. We owe much to Frances E. Willard who encouraged us on to the bicycle and into the world. In her honor, I suggest you throw on your most comfortable clothes, hop on your bike and ride over to the W.C.T.U. headquarters at 1730 Chicago Avenue in Evanston. On the same property, you will see Rest Cottage, the Willard family home. Now an historical landmark and newly restored, it sits in quiet Victorian dignity amid its glass and brick neighbors. Its quiet facade, deceptively innocent, hides the electric energy and accomplishments of one woman far ahead of her time.

Inside, you will also see Gladys. She rests under the stairs and looks like many of us Aging Activists — worn out in some places and fraying in others, but still standing proud! Her bell still works. I asked permission and then rang it once to hear her speak. Then, I rang it again in celebration of the power two good women can exert on the world when they put their minds to it.

## Clara Johnson

### Florence and James

Florence and James came into the world while the Twenties were still roaring. I'm sure my father never made bathtub gin — no bathtub — or frequented speakeasies. Nor did my mother ever wear short dresses or flapper beads or dance the Charleston. But life was easier before the Depression, when there was a decent market for farm products and they had only two children — Florence and James.

The best toys our family had were bought for Florence and James. Florence had a tricycle, which we called "pedal," and James rode a wooden saddle horse mounted on wheels. They had first use of the little red wagon, which survived the hauling of all later-arriving Johnsons.

One of our earliest family photos is a front yard picture of Florence "caring" for an unseen "baby" lying in the little wicker buggy. Bald-headed little James is holding to the foot of the buggy and flashing his winning grin at Florence. Two little kids forging a lasting bond with each other.

I was an intruder. An aggressive one, I've been told. I was never to worm my way into Florence and James' special relationship.

Florence was loyal to James, of whom I learned to be wary. He would thump me with his fists or a handy toy if I didn't conform to whatever rules he laid down. And thump me again for being a "crybaby." Florence wasn't a hitter. At times, she gave me good and useful advice, which I resented needing, but I didn't win her approval. I was "selfish," "too rowdy," and I couldn't get along with James.

James' discipline made me devious. I'd play with his toys when he wasn't around, then deny that I'd touched them. He'd tell mother that I was "telling stories" and Florence would confirm this. They were allies.

I remember James telling me I was "too bad" to ever go to school. I proved him wrong. I went to school. But he said I walked so slow that I'd make them late. So Florence would pull me along and James would march in front, setting the pace.

I may have been "good enough" to go to school, but, according to James, I still wasn't "good." He'd tell Mother that I got out of my seat when I wasn't supposed to, that I whispered to Vera, and turned around to look at Junior.

I began to watch James. He turned around to whisper to Harold and he would put his feet in the aisle, where he wasn't supposed to have them. When I'd tell Mother about *that,* James would deny it. Florence would confirm James' stories about me but not my stories about him. Then James would berate me and hit me for being such a "tattletale." Florence never told on him when he did this. They were still allies.

I turned to Louis and Zella. They liked the games I made up and loved to hear me read. I would lie between them on the semi-reclining couch and become a bear or rabbit, if that's what the story called for.

James had a winning personality. He was good at games, playing and creating them. The other kids, the Langes, the Krueger boys, and even the Edwards girls liked him. Miss Bloom liked him, too. She would praise his good work and listen to his long explanations about things. Louis and Zella liked him, too. He didn't play much with them, but he'd tickle them and tell funny stories.

It never bothered James to acknowledge that Florence was smart. He'd dismiss *my* good report cards because I wasn't taking "hard subjects," like he and Florence were. He'd laugh about my arithmetic mistakes and ridicule my penmanship. And, always, tell our folks about my every misdeed.

James wasn't surprised when Florence graduated third of all eighth-graders in Macoupin County, because he "knew she was smart." When he graduated the next year, he wasn't in the high ten, but Miss Bloom told him he'd done "very well" on the county exams. The next year, he joined Florence and the Denby girls on their two-mile walk to the bus which carried them to high school.

Two years later, it was my turn to study for the county exams. We had a different teacher, a Mr. Denby. I liked him, but I knew he wasn't keeping me after school to drill me, the way Miss Bloom had kept Florence and James. I was afraid that I wouldn't do well on the exams,  that James would be proven right. That I might even fail them.

What a relief when, in early July, Mr. Denby sent me a postcard telling me I had passed everything — with good grades. He wrote, "Nothing is yet known about the high ten, but I think you have a chance to make it."

"If you make high ten, I'll buy you a twenty-five dollar wristwatch, " James scoffed.

When Mr. Denby drove over to tell me that I was on the high ten — *seventh* on the high ten — I crowed and demanded that James give me that twenty-five dollar watch. James probably didn't have twenty-five dollars, but, even if he had, I knew he'd never spend it on me.

When girls go to high school, they wear lipstick. I didn't have any lipstick, but Kresge's did, and I had a dollar. I wasn't reckless enough to spend the whole dollar on lipstick, but I could get Tangee Orange for ten cents. I'd rather have bought red, but that cost more.

It seemed like, every day, on the way to the bus, James would make fun of my lipstick. "Wipe the orange juice off your mouth, " he'd say. Then he and Beulah Denby would just laugh and laugh. James had stopped punching me, but the things he would say could hurt as much as a punch.

James graduated from high school and started to college. But Pearl Harbor had been bombed and all the boys were registering for the draft. Before his number came up, James volunteered for the Air Force. He trained first at the cooking and baking school, but he didn't liked that work. He gave up his stripes to enter bombardier school.

I graduated from high school and went to Blackburn, a junior college, and, in the absence of all male students, became an assistant to Dr. Witmer, the chemistry professor. After I got my Associate of Arts degree, Dr. Witmer recommended me for a laboratory position in Peoria. I got the job, after signing a statement agreeing to give up my position when the young men returned from the war.

During these years, James would come home on furloughs. We had a better camera by then and took more pictures. There were pictures of James with the entire family, with James and our parents, with James standing between his two brothers, and one with his four sisters. In that one, he's standing between Florence and Zella, an arm around each of them. They have their arms around him. I'm standing a tiny distance from Zella, with my arms hanging at my sides, and Mary Ann is standing in front of James.

One day in February, Aunt Opal called me with the bad news. James' plane had been shot down in the Pacific and the entire crew was listed as "Missing in Action."

For the first time, I saw my father cry. Mother would join us in a circle, cry, and try to pray. Florence was so painfully sad. Louis, Zella, William and Mary Ann were silently grieving. I was numb and conscience-stricken. I'd had a lot of bad feelings toward James and they'd never been resolved. Not once during his furloughs had I hugged him and told him I was glad to see him. How would he have received such a demonstration? Had he been waiting for an overture which hadn't come? I'll never know.

Florence lives in Florida now. She makes light of the two serious operations she's had and says she feels fine. We write to each other. She tells me about her children and grandchildren and about the trips she takes. I sent her a few family stories I'd written. She answered that she "enjoyed the stories," but couldn't remember any of the events I'd reported.

In my next letter after that, I asked her to write some stories she did remember. She replied that, at one time, she had wanted to become a writer, but, now, she knew she never would.

**Mary  Hanford**

Goblets

In my kitchen goblets stand
in scattered rows. When I first set
the highballs my parents left me,
they hung in the back, wedding gifts
to that Harvard lawyer, shattered with drink,
who, tall and costly, married a preacher's daughter,
three months pregnant. Those two swilled scotch
and grenadine when I was five crouching beneath
the blue clock atop a columned mantle.

Dime store tumblers, all that remain
of a marriage anonymous as a third-floor
notions department. Grandmother's monogram
impressed on wine glasses at the top.
She presided at a mahogany table,
flaunting both breasts missing,
still soaring. She counseled me
to roll money under my skirts.

And ruby sherbets, resplendent
in crimson, repose on the ledge.
Helmeted light glances from oval epaulets,
shooting from rifles of carved crystal,
ricocheting off the memory of a cousin,
who at thirteen, swept me up the stairs.
Like me, the clear tumblers are indistinct
against juice and olive jars.

Only the red snifters remain,
saluting brilliant blood bonds —
a smudged memorial.

## Spell

"Don't plant potatoes by the dark
of the moon; Sleep North for twins;
August sparrows mean an early frost," drone
wind-woven matrons, shedding crocheted
half-moons into corn husks.

"I will lie with him," whispers
my inner forecast.

As spaniels' thickened fur
augers a bitter winter,
I see those hob-nailed lacemakers
toss their shuttle,
scalloping a lemon bunting
to enclose us.

## Bonnie Tunick

I am afraid
we have run our course,
my love.
Sometimes
when I am with you,
I am inclined
to hold a mirror to my mouth
to make sure
I am still alive.

When her ex suggested
they get back together
nearly a year after leaving
for a younger woman,
Sophia responded
with all the respect
she could muster.

## Etta L. Worthington

### Swimming

Sometimes you forget
*Jason don't tease your sister like that   You know I've told
you a thousand times*
He doesn't listen   None of them listen now   They used
to In the beginning
Well it's no wonder you forget
You want to forget   You want to not know that they are
here these three parasites these three leeches sucking off your
blood
Children Mother always said having children was the
most fulfilling the most rewarding job in the world and that
you weren't a woman until you'd had one   She'd always feel
sorry for those women who couldn't   She never let it pass
through her mind that some women might not have
children because they didn't want children
She had six of you   How could she have felt that way
having six human parasites sucking from her for years and
years
She's dead now and you never got to ask her but you
wondered   How could she have liked it watching her life
drain into all of you and growing older and older and less
and less
How could she not have wanted to forget
It's crazy maybe but sometimes you still find yourself
astounded when you look around and see the hockey sticks
dropped in the family room and the mounds of laundry in
the basement and the pictures taped to the fridge Well
sometimes you find yourself shaking your head as if you've
just awakened from a 20 year sleep and can't believe what
has happened
*Jason I told you before you can't have your friends over
until you've cleaned your room   That's it and I don't want you
asking me again*

God Where has the time gone   This isn't you   This dreary housewife worn ragged with the demands of three children and a husband whose highest function in life seems to be that of being chauffeur   Comes in front of cook

Damn   They're driving you crazy   You wish summer were over   You count the days   Twenty one days left   Twenty one long days since Bob said you weren't going to the lake this summer for a week like you usually do   His family has a place but he's not talking to his parents this year and so you have to sit out the rest of August at home

Petty fights   He's always picking them with his family or you or the kids and when it's the kids you have to try and mediate   Sometimes you wish he'd be here when they're all picking on each other so you didn't have to always be the bad guy and send them to their room or sit them in the corner or ground them

Michelle is of grounding age   She's thirteen and you can tell she hates you most of the time   She goes around glaring at you if she looks at you at all and you're certain that there's absolutely nothing in the world you could do that would please her other than giving her your credit card and dropping her off at the mall for a day   Even then she'd be mad at you by the time she got home you're sure

You ground her fairly often   And then she's even more sullen and you wish to God that teenage years would speed by faster than they seem to be

But that's not true   They are speeding by and you just aren't acknowledging it because you try to ignore your birthday every year but 35 arrived and you weren't ready for it and you're half the way to 40 now

God where has the time gone

*Yes* you yell to Jason *I'll go out with you in ten minutes If you have your room cleaned*

Brent wants to go too so you tell him to go upstairs and go to the bathroom and get his suit on and by the time he's ready it'll probably be time to get out there

*Michelle* you yell to her *Do you want to go swimming*

She doesn't answer but that's normal but you figure she'll show up

You might as well enjoy the pool too you decide so you go upstairs to get your suit on  You probably won't swim that much but you can sunbathe

Ah yes  You remember sunbathing  That's what you'd do instead of studying for finals

Lay out at Oak Street beach and watch the guys walk by and hope they were noticing you  Or hope some one of them would stumble on you playing Frisbee and it happened  Bob stumbled on you and you started talking and before you knew it he'd ask you out and you agreed and that was the start of everything

You look at yourself in the mirror  That's unlike you  You used to do it all the time but not any more  Three kids and zillions of stretch marks and you don't like looking at yourself anymore and probably Bob doesn't either which is why you only make love in the dark anymore

But you look now and you sort of squint and everything changes and you think you don't look that much different than you used to so you go and get the two piece swimming suit Bob gave you for an anniversary present 10 years ago and put it on

You'll wear a robe over it when you go down  The kids have never seen you in it and you want to break them in gently  Or maybe it's breaking yourself in  You're not used to exposing this much of yourself  You thought of this as a two piece suit but after you have it on you think bikini is a better label for it  You're wearing a bikini and you haven't done that since you were in your 20s

You squint and you look much better  You squint and there are no stretch marks no pot belly that you can't suck in anymore no varicose veins no saddlebags

You squint and look and you're 19 again  and you're getting ready to go to the beach for the afternoon

You're 19 again and you're full of energy and hope  And there's nothing that's impossible

You're 19 again   You are standing on the edge of life waiting to jump into the stream to swim like hell with all the other struggling bodies   You are 19 looking downstream to see where you'll end up   The possibilities are endless   The sky is the limit You can do anything you want   You are free

*Mother you look ridiculous in that thing   You're not going out in the yard with that on   What would Dad say*

You are hurtled shoved smashed back into reality   She is glaring at you and you glare back and she stomps from the room   You wonder how long she watched you in front of the mirror and if she had any inkling of what you were thinking

She despises you that's obvious

She would despise you even more if she knew you never quite remember that you've gone past the beginning   You haven't internalized the fact that life is whipping past you

At 19 you were free and you like to forget that all that has changed and so you march downstairs and out into the yard and Jason laughs at you and you don't care

You tell them to be careful and no splashing and no diving off the side   It's only four feet deep and they could get hurt if they tried diving

You ease yourself into the above ground pool that your husband had installed in the back yard last year and it's hot and the water feels good

Not so good though   Somehow even when you yell at them those two boys find a way of splashing so you get out of the pool and stretch out on your beach towel

You close your eyes and yes you are 19 again and you can hear the sound of a Frisbee game happening and any minute now a stray Frisbee will come flying your way and he'll stumble over you going after it   Then he'll mumble excuse me and you'll open your eyes and smile and  look in his eyes and he'll ask your name and it will start all over again

**Ann Stotts**

Daughter Rite

for Michelle Citron

"A woman is her mother
That's the main thing"
-- Anne Sexton

1.

The passage is there is no rite of passage.
mother and daughter,
the enduring pair,
even as you grow to despise
the body you grow into,
her voice through the telephone wire
your shaken own,
even as you:
                read her diary
                find her romance novels
                step on the crack


that broke her mother's back.
Your masquerade of femininity.
childhood scenes
played out in endless film loops:
birthday girl, swan rides,
naked at the sink


roses              carriage          walking


In identical Easter dress,
a perversion of twins,
your stride matches hers
slowed down,
You smile
        as father shoots all of you.

2.

Baby sister got tied down
and stabbed, inoculates lately
with pills and married men.
even with her, the angry
intimacy, so many
where to gos, what should we dos,
so many ways to make a fruit salad.

Out in some ocean,
escaped through an upper bedroom window,
the daughters tread water
call out to one another
weave exotic fishing nets.

Back on the beach,
the mother's mouth wide open--

Native Resistance

1.

You look, your eyes
as big as runaway
horses, calculating
as 35 millimeters.
On the side of the road
my ears ring from honks
meant to compliment
their owners.

I mean my solitary walk
to say this is not your
street, your turf,
your native land.

2.

Suffragettes were known
for their crazy quilts.

3.

The poet revolutionary
explodes into the 15-year
old prostitute, notices
a bruise bloom violet
on her thigh.
The moment regretted
in its consummation?

4.

A  pregnant woman
in an elevator
full of men
is an island.
Two angry women
in a kitchen

are in hiding.
Three women
holding hands
in the middle
of a street
can stop traffic.

**Linda Mowry**

The Spare Room
(an excerpt from a novel in progress)

Addie Black bought a house. It was a good time to get
into real estate. The house was a solid investment, a very
good buy indeed. It was sound, needed no major work
before she moved in. The house was just waiting for
someone with the patience to undo thoughtless remodeling,
ready for someone with an eye for proportion who would
pull away the acoustical tiles and patch the high plaster
ceiling. Someone who would unblock the fireplace, strip the
oak woodwork,  rediscover the hardwood floors, give the
kitchen back its character. It was waiting for Addie Black.

The best thing, for Addie, was the fact that no one had
questioned the purchase. For she knew that regardless of
condition, she would have had that house. After all, it had
waited for her.

Naturally, she didn't dwell on it. Not that she
pretended she bought the place because it was sound, and
just the right size, and interest rates were good, and she was
established at the University. She simply left undusted her
brain's equivalent of the back corner of the guest room
closet, where this knowledge lived.

The thought sat quietly on the dark shelf while Addie
Black gradually made the house hers in a way that was
characteristically practical; that is to say, reduced to
research, numbers, formulae:

"Wallpapers of this period were typically patterned
with...."

"No, ma'am, we couldn't get it back to you before...."

"Plasterer — 16 hours @ $18.00/hour...."

The walls were steamed and scraped and painted and
papered. The odor of the 1940's was removed along with
the carpets. Her bedroom received her furniture with an ease
which would have made her tremble if she hadn't been so
busy with the plumbers and the door refinishers. Eventually

the chipped enamel kitchen sink was replaced with a stainless steel one of the same old-fashioned dimensions. The ugly modern carpet gave way to equally practical vinyl of fittingly classic design. The hall's cacophony of texture and pattern was finally stripped back to clean lines, soft colors, and glowing wood — a warm welcome for resident and visitors alike. The small bedroom at the front of the house became her study. the day after the Audubon prints were hung, she sat at her commodious desk and could not remember what the room had looked like before.

The house was hers.

It was the place her dorm room should have been the day she went to Professor Williams' office to discuss the "problem" with her research. It was the place her apartment should have been when her parents died. The place she should have been able to go home to after helping Yvonne with Karen when Jason was born.

During the two years it took to accomplish all this, Addie gave little thought to the other bedroom, which was even smaller than her study. While restorations were being done elsewhere in the house, it was convenient to have the spare room to store furniture. When everything else was done, the walls of this room were steamed and scraped and patched and smoothed and simply painted white. The floor, gleaming and bare, had been refinished with the other upstairs rooms. She thought she might get a television and put it in this unused space.

She was barreling through the department store after work one day, needing only vacuum cleaner bags, when she became caught in the linen department, lost in clouds of white flowers and recollection.


She hadn't known, until she went back to the farm, that she'd been avoiding it. The Bloomington campus was such a long way from Ross Township, and she had been busy her first year as full professor. But driving north out of Fort

Wabash that August morning, she continually fell below the speed limit. She asked herself why she and Maynard Wisner couldn't discuss the rental of the land next year by phone. When she turned from the US highway to the paved county road she felt such dread that she had to admit it. She just didn't want to see the place now that the house was gone. She and Tony had grown up in it, their parents had grown old and died peacefully, if somewhat prematurely, in it. Somehow Yvonne was tied up in it, too, maybe because Thanksgiving dinner at the old house was where she first met her future sister-in-law.

She slowed for the turn onto the gravel road, reminding herself that she was tired, that it was silly to give in to so much musing when she was exhausted by a week of shopping, cooking, laundry, chasing after four-year-old Karen, and helping with the baby. Not that she had minded. It was worth it to see Yvonne bounce back.

Addie turned, following inevitably the familiar route. past Bredemeyers' where mucky yards and manicured emerald lawn opened up views to the left, past the wall of Ott's multiflora roses, anemic with gravel dust. The swing right into her own drive was automatic.

She had known, had feared, it would look different. But this —— this was *different*. Unexpected. Beautiful. White flowers billowed over each side of the drive, an impossible fantasy, simultaneously peaceful and exuberant, welcoming and — different. Addie Black knew this farm and this drive in every kind of summer: cool and dry, hot and wet, vice versa. She had never seen this spread of white on green. High as the car, Queen Anne's lace drifted ahead of her. From near the ground and as tall as the wild carrot, sweet clover swayed shamelessly, gracefully. The car crawled as if resigned to finding its own way in, while Addie spotted yarrow and scatterings of fleabane. Campion, here and there, nodded as if too modest to flaunt its whiter white. And everywhere, filling in as the florist uses babies' breath, was a profusion of Whitlow grass.

Addie Black braked. The past was gone, like Atlantis. Behind her, frothy wave stretched to meet foaming crest. Before her, Maynard Wisner's soy beans rippled gently.

"Sweet, isn't it?"

Addie blinked herself back to the present. She glanced from the saleswoman back to the display. "Yes," she answered.

Both drapes and spread were done in the remarkable print, the white and cream dainty, yet dominating on the soft greens. She was glad they were tailored plainly; ruffles would have been cloying. The spread was turned back to show coordinating solid color sheets of the soothing paler green, piped with the darker shade.

"May I help you?"

"No. No, thank you." Addie hurried away to get her vacuum cleaner bags.

She thought she had forgotten the print. But that night, on her way to her study, thinking only of the journals and papers in her bulging briefcase, she looked into the spare room and saw the green and white print hanging at the window, covering a new mattress on the carved oak headboard from the old house. Addie decided she didn't need a television room after all.

Once purchased and in place, the drapes and spread looked as good as she had imagined they would. But the small room felt unfinished.

Yvonne loved it. Jason asked if he could initiate the room as her first overnight guest. He came down Saturday morning to prepare the waffles which were his specialty since junior high Home Ec, and declared the room good. Yet Addie often found herself standing in the doorway, wondering if she should rearrange the furniture, even though the room was so small that the bed and the little gateleg table could not be placed any other way. She bought the green sheets to go under the green and white spread and told herself the room was done.

Shirley Exeter and her daughter and son-in-law stopped, bringing her pumpkins, squash, and Ross Township news. Shirley insisted on the "fifty-cent tour" although she'd seen the house before. She enthused again over the fireplace, the kitchen cupboards, the stained glass window. And especially the guest room.

When they were gone Addie stopped to look again, casting her most critical eye over the furnishings. It lacked nothing. Yet....She smoothed a fold in the drapes. She held the corner of a picture frame while she checked that it was straight. The room wanted something but she could not put her finger on it.

She saw them again the very next weekend, on a Conservation League hike. Addie stood on the periphery of conversation as Shirley's daughter quizzed the Greenfield girl.

"What do you mean, Nicki can't be there? Someone has to take care of you after the hearing."

Addie liked Elizabeth Greenfield's dry response, "I'll manage somehow, Rebecca." She liked very much the young woman Elizabeth had become, in spite of Addie's own predictions. Addie had been so disappointed when Helen, the bright, pretty neighbor girl Addie had always looked up to, came back from college to live at home and teach at Ross Center. She could have achieved so much more. Helen had dropped even further in Addie's estimation when she married a farmer who simply moved in with Helen and her parents. Learning — by then through her mother's letters — that Helen and Harold had no plans to move to a house of their own after their daughter was born, Addie declared (if only to herself) that the only child in a household of four doting adults would be spoiled worthless or pampered to incompetence.

Yet Elizabeth was neither. The more Addie heard about her, the more she admired her. It took a special woman to be the summer camp director in whom a nine year old who was being sexually abused confided. It took even more to be the person who did something about it.

Addie found herself the straggler and hurried over the muddy trail to catch up with Elizabeth.

"What are we missing by walking so fast?" Elizabeth asked.

"Nothing. I'm just slow." They both spotted some fungus and stopped for a closer look, releasing a rotten odor when they pulled their boots out of the bog to return to the path.

Addie thought of her guest room print. Sweet. "This hearing you have — why don't you stay with me afterward. I have room. I'll be happy to give you a meal. To listen, if you feel like talking. Leave you alone if you don't."

Elizabeth paused mid-stride to look down at her, assessing. Addie halted, too, wondering if she should repeat the invitation. If simply issuing it had been presumptuous. Why would this young woman want her company?

"Thank you," Elizabeth replied. "I'd like that."

Addie wondered then if she should invite Yvonne, who was so much better at tea and sympathy. But she didn't know how to engineer it, so it was just she and Elizabeth who ate the spinach omelet and contemplated the flames in the fireplace while they discussed the Hoosier Conservation League, the Ft. Wabash Audubon Society and "Elizabeth's girls."

She had gone by the time Addie came home from the University next day. Addie looked in to find the guest room exactly as it was before Elizabeth had stayed. Except that now it felt complete. She cocked her head, involuntarily, as if hearing the last piece of the puzzle which was her house pressed into place. Addie almost snorted at herself as she pushed the thought to the back of the closet shelf.

**Andrea  Cuchetto**

Baking

I ate a wommon today
    browned too brown, her hand reaching
    forward for what she will touch
    & her foot browned, too browned —
    the last, the past, her foot
    still in it;
    too brown browned to qualify for
    the 1950s third edition first
    printing Betty Crocker Picture
    Book instructions that called
    for a "delicate brown"

I ate her hand first
    then I bit into her browned too brown sugary foot
    & chewed my way down from the top of her head
    to her shoulder
    nibbled to the very last, her toes.
    I hold them in my left hand as I write
    & peer closely at the
    shade of brown I could leave alone, this bit, this last bite
    her toes, a "delicate brown" — so much a part of a foot
    they could be a mistake drop crumb on the cookie
    sheet, an accident

With a tiny push of my finger I eat the delicate brown
    browned
    toes & touch my tongue so that I might feel & taste
    & remember I am alive

I ate a wommon today
    a wommon I would not give away
    (failed to meet expectations again)
    & she was altogether the best "mistake" I've ever
    made.

## Carol Gloor

### The Housewife's Autumn Hymn

No tumor can root in me
while I chlorine scrub the sink:
no bones grow brittle while I lemon polish
the wood
with my little cat's tongue.
I iron away wrinkles and sweep
the crumbs of chaos and stale bacon
from underneath the kitchen radiator.
I feather my nest with
fluffy towels, laundered curtains
and sweet vacuumed rugs,
pack my jowls with home baked
bran muffins plump
with swollen raisins.
I brush my upholstered furniture
'til my fur shines
and paint my dingy walls
'til my nails gleam, lengthen, harden.
My windowsills and doorknobs
are free from finger marks,
my paperbacks are alphabetized,
my shelves papered,
my cups hang from hooks,
my arms crocheted with doilies.
My mirrors, windows, eyes
glisten in twilight.
Soup simmers on my heart stove.
My ironing board stands
straight, high and ready,
like my tail.
Winter approaches.
It is good and safe
to love me.

## Lesson One

Jim, the dime store manager,
said don't pinch your titties,
as I lugged boxes of Slinkies
up the 1961 stairs five
minutes before closing.
I punched out and he patted
my ass, wanting me,
he said, to meet his girlfriend
Wanda, who, it turned out,
was old as my mother,
dyed white hair,
skin Avon brown,
red glass ring
on her middle finger
and plastic gold sandals
on her varicose feet.

She'd lost two teeth
and sang in bars for a living,
voice rough as her bucket hands,
and laughed like a river
as she leaned toward me
in the backseat convertible
while Jim peed
into the vacant lot.

Listen, she whispered,
sweet with bourbon,
disfigured with empathy,
I try to help him,
it's been so hard
for him, so hard.

I was sixteen.
Lesson One.

**Charise Studesville**

## Same Old Mess

The crowd of teens cheered from the sidewalk as papiermache-covered platforms floated by. Almost the only Black faces in the crowd were the football players who presided over the convertibles in the parade. They waved to the mass of white faces who chanted the players' names like some pseudo-religious mantra. Aside from the players, there was a small group of Black students gathered amidst the crowd. And one lone Black cheerleader. Though she was so light-skinned she was regularly mistaken for "just another white girl."

At the parade's end, the students scattered into the streets and throughout the school courtyard. Cara, the Black cheerleader, headed back inside the school, making her way to the bathroom. Three other girls from the group of Black students along the parade route followed some distance behind her.

Cara was already inside a stall when the other girls came into the bathroom discussing someone who, as one put it, "...thinks she's so damn cute."

Cara heard another girl's voice chime in, "Well, we're gonna just have to 'fix' her up a little. We'll let her know we got 'Miss Thang's' number." [Other voices joined in laughter.]

Cara couldn't help dipping into their conversation as she smoothed out the pleats in the skirt of her uniform and flushed the toilet. She recognized Gloria's voice. They had some words last year, but it was long-ago history at this point. [She wondered who they were talking about.]

The door to the toilet stall stuck, almost like someone was holding it shut on purpose. But she didn't see any feet under the stall door when she checked. She gave the door another shove. Bam. It opened.

The moment Cara stepped onto the dirty pink floor tile, she felt a rush of pain shoot from her neck into her head.

Someone had yanked her foot-long braid, snapping her head back like a PEZ candy dispenser. Before she could react, Gloria was standing in front of her, smiling.

"I say we give the little yella bitch a trim," Gloria said, as she held a BIC lighter in front of Cara's eyes, still holding onto her hair. "Or maybe we should work on that face."

"Are you crazy?" Cara screeched, struggling to get away from both the lighter-wielding Gloria and Pam. who was holding her from behind. Her eyes pleaded with Geneva, who was standing in the corner, fixing her lipstick in the mirror.

Pam spun Cara around, allowing Gloria to singe the bottom inch of the braid with the lighter as Tracy, Cara's best friend. rushed in. "What the fuck is going on?" Tracy demanded.

"Oh, just taking care of some unfinished bizness is all, " Gloria answered.

"Showing little 'Miss It' that her shit ain't all that great," added Pam,  as she shoved Cara into Tracy. Cara ended up in a heap on the floor, still stunned.

Gloria and Pam laughed their way out of the bathroom. Geneva, following, simply smirked at Cara and Tracy before letting the door close behind her.

"I don't believe this shit, " Cara said, half crying and half laughing.

"What happened?" her friend asked as she helped Cara up from the dingy floor. "You know, I had a feeling something like this was coming. That's why I came looking for you."

"Whattaya mean, you 'had a feeling'?" Cara demanded, incredulously. "So I did something to deserve this shit?"

"Girl, don't be stupid. You know that's not what I meant," Tracy responded, helping Cara fix the singed ends of hair sticking out of the rubber band. "I just know that someone like Gloria looks at you, and she's going to blame the most obvious difference she sees between the two of you for why you 'have', and she doesn't."

Cara just stood, numb, listening to Tracy tell her what she already knew, but didn't like to see. Ever since she could remember, there was always some darker-skinned girl who swore she, Cara, lived the "ain't-got-no-blues-'cause-I'm-too light-to-lose" life.

"I've heard the other girls whispering about you," Tracy admitted. She didn't add that sometimes they even questioned Tracy about why a "real"— meaning brown-skinned — sister would hang out with "that little yella bitch." "Are you okay?"

Cara looked faraway. Before she answered, she let out a deep sigh. "Yeah, I'm alright. Tired. Just tired."

And with that she slowly gathered up her pompons and headed for the door.


Still in her uniform, Tracy approached the steps of the well-kept house on the city's south side. One thing she knew for sure was that she had to leave the day's events behind her if she wanted to get out of the house without her grandmother catching on that anything was wrong. She just hoped the fix-up job she and Tracy had attempted on her hair had done the trick.

"Hi, Grandma, it's Cara, " she yelled as she laid down the mail on the coffee table in the living room.

As she walked through to the dining room she ran her fingers over the tops of the picture frames that lined the wood veneer of the old television console. Funny, but before today, she had never noticed that all the women in the pictures looked just like her. As if someone had dressed her up in old clothes like at one of those amusement park picture studios. They were all light-skinned, with long hair. And all the men were "Dark Gables," with rich brown skin over handsome faces and strong bodies. Almost like some unspoken rule had existed in their family that deemed all handsome brown men were only to marry pretty yellow women. The pictures bothered her, but she didn't allow herself think about it long enough to decide why.

Smelling her way to the kitchen, Cara peeped into the full pots simmering on the stove. Steaming peppery greens in one. Juicy fried corn in another. And her favorite was on the counter nearby — buttery, cinnamon-laced peach cobbler fresh from the oven. "You gotta give it to the old broad. she can cook her ass off."

"What was that?" Grandma responded, giving one of her scolding looks as she came out of the back room.

"Why is it you can hear everything I say when you're out of the room, but I can sit right next to you and it's 'Can't hear you. Don't have my hearing aid in.'"

"Alright, girly, being so sassy with your grandmother. You're not too big for me to take a switch to your behind." She added, "Your barely-covered behind, if I do say so myself."

"Grandma, now you know you could never hurt your little darlin'," Cara teased as she reached over to give her grandmother a big hug, ignoring the last part of her comment.

"You and your sisters, ya'll think you're cute," Grandma replied as she playfully swatted Cara away. "But none of ya'll could hold a stick to me when I was young."

Cara saw what was coming and whispered under her breath, " I had some beautiful legs."

"Girl, I had some beautiful legs, "Grandma said. "I know I got a picture somewhere," she added, heading toward the closet to get one of her shoe boxes filled with pictures. But she turned around to make another point and noticed Cara's hair, grabbing at the end of the braid, all jagged at the end from being burned.

"Lord have mercy, child, looks like your hair caught on fire," she said, sniffing the braid. "Now don't go trying to tell me some craziness like this is from a pressing comb or something. 'Cause ain't none of the women in our family ever had to put no fire to their hair — chemical or otherwise."

Cara went to the sink and began washing and snapping the fresh green beans piled in the metal colander, putting the snapped ends into one of the big black and white speckled cooking pots Grandma used. "It's no big deal...I just got into it with some girls at school is all."

"You got into a fight over some boy or something? Oh, Lord, please don't tell me a granddaughter of mine's been laying down with no mens. I just can't hear nothing like that, not with my blood pressure." Grandma sat down on her black and metal foldout stool while holding her hand to her chest.

"No, Grandma," Cara answered, fighting a smile. " There's just some girls at school who seem to have it in for me or something."

"No boy, huh? They must be some little dark-skinned things, then, weren't they?"

Cara was only partially surprised. "They just don't know me, really. That's all. And they think I'm stuck up or something. You know, when people don't know you and you're quiet at first like I am ..."

"What'd they say to you?"

Not wanting to answer, but knowing she had no choice, Cara told her grandmother everything that had happened.

"Uhm, uhm-uhm. Same old mess. After all these years."

Cara tried to change the subject by asking whether Grandma wanted all the beans snapped , or if she was saving some for Sunday dinner. But the old woman wasn't having it.

"Yep, they was jealous alright. Women are like that. Especially those dark ones."

"Now that is just an ugly thing to say. Especially coming from a supposedly good Christian woman."

"Well, maybe so. But it's the truth. Did I ever tell you about the time I was working at the five-and-dime down home?

"Yeah, I was a pretty little thing, like I told you. And I was just as sweet as could be. No more than about seventeen, waiting on tables. Well, in comes this evil-looking, dark-skinned woman. She was a regular. Always mean and mad at the world. But she usually set at old

Crooked-Teeth Corrine's station. Well, I went over to ask her 'Could I get you anything?', real nice and sweet. and she just looked up at me, curling those lips of hers into a smile and says, 'Yes, you could git me a knife, so's I can slice up that pretty yella face of yours. Bet all the fellas wouldn't be doin' no talking 'bout Pretty Polly then, would they?'"

"Oh, my God," Cara started. But seeing Grandma's disapproving look, she adjusted, "Gosh. Oh, my Gosh."

"Then, just like that, she gits up and leaves. But just as she got past me, she turns around and says, 'Watch now, yella.' Had your granddaddy to walk me home from work for a long while, just to be on the lookout for her crazy self."

"And you never found out why she said that to you? Why she just happened to pick on you?"

"Oh, I knew that right away. That's what I been trying to tell you. Those dark-skinned girls, they're just jealous. ''Cept for that little dark-skinned friend of yours."

"*Tracy*, Grandma. You know her name is Tracy."

"Ya'll do seem to truly be friends. And that's real nice, you know. 'Cause when I was young, they was all too jealous. With my pretty legs and all, I mean."

"Yes, ma'am, " Cara sighed. " I'm sure that's what it was."

## Patricia Richmond

### Horse 7/10
### A Present for Michael

Silence over this etching in the midst of the
Jangling of artists;
The search was over.

I calmly studied it in the mayhem,
      hands clasped behind me.
We were here.

Its dark power
Reminded me of you

      Your hands, classic, primitive, all possibility

Its neck arched, noble

      Your flanks sleek with sweat

Smooth in spite of the
Ragged power of strokes

      Not the skill but the patience it took to comb out
      Your stormy hair

It will look well on a contrasting wall in your house
I have never seen.
It will make you remember in spite of yourself

Congratulations on your marriage.

## Bonnie Tunick

Once or twice a year
when reality gets ugly,
Sharon calls in sick
after the kids leave for school,
sleeps till noon,
then turns on the soaps
and waits for the pizza man
to arrive.

She plans trips to the Bahamas
and counts loads of laundry
when her husband makes love to her.
He is never with her on the beach
drinking Mai Tais.
She is no longer washing
his Fruit of the Looms.

**Wendy Heller**

Being together


we drive in your car, or mine
mostly you do dishes, I cook
we take showers, drink tea
mostly, the days wind through our nights

I have faulted you
shedding your tears
like an outgrown skin

you have slammed the lids of your eyes
and left home
never to return

still we find ourselves
squared off
in the kitchen
dancing
and fencing

## Sleeping Alone

the house is
        my skin.
thunder laps at
        my foundation
rain kicks at
        my door
it enters,
        and enters,
                and enters
in places I can't see
        or cover

cloaked by night
        and bedclothes
I am exactly as visible
as a house, this
house, awaiting
the man who is coming.

the man who is
        coming,
who enters   who is
entering      boots on
        the stairs      thunder in
the halls, whose shadow
        blossoms, shatters eggshell walls,
gets into my
        skin

my skin.
open in places
my house can't see,
can't cover

## Spartan Jar

Here is my story.
At twenty-four
I was as brown
as the baked clay
of our molded pots.
The harsh light
battled the colors
until I was as faded
an image
as you see now,
as essential a form.

Our husbands
were visitors in our lives,
as remote
a story as
Olympus.
We labored together, our hands
in the burning soil.

Most of my life
seems as still
as the sun at noon
until a soft cool night,
when time passed
as swiftly as
the shadows
where I took her.

# Kathryn Brettinger

## Choices

When my brother Bert was six, Ma dragged him out of the sand pile, dressed him up in his new blue shirt, smacked his cowlick down against his head, and drove him to the town school. All us older kids went tagging along for the ride. We scrambled into our decrepit station wagon — Ma and me and Bert in front, Bob, Myrna and the twins in the middle, and three crates of Buff Orphingtons in the back. Buff Orphingtons are chickens. And these particular chickens belonged to Ma.

All us kids hated the darn things. They used to wake us up in the morning with their clucking, and every once in a while they'd all gang up to chase and flap whoever got stuck with the chore of taking them their mash. They loved Ma, though, in their dumb Buff Orphington way, and she liked them too.

Every year we got new chicks, and every year she would take each ball of yellow fluff and give it a name. This year she thought we would like having the birds named after us. My namesake, Vinnie, grew up brown-speckled, cross-eyes and used to take sun-stroke when the temperature went above ninety, and would run around the chicken yard for an hour at a stretch in a mad frenzy. Bert and me had our own name for Vinnie. We called her the Dumb Cluck.

Ma just didn't keep the darn things for pets though. Good heavens, she didn't need a couple of dozen squawking, unreasonable chicken-pets with seven squawking, unreasonable kids.

Ma kept them for the hen money. Every year the poultry market man, Mr. Van Vooren, would look over the summer's crop of birds and offer her a price. All us kids would watch Ma screw up her face, point out some outstanding feature of this or that particular clucking fool, and up the number a notch or two. Then Mr. Van Vooren would hem and haw and poke around in the crates for a minute — and name another number somewhere in the middle. Ma would narrow her eyes and pause dramatically. Then they'd shake hands and it would be all over.

That was Ma's hen money. And it was really hers, too. The money from the field crops went to the family. The money from the truck garden went to the Rainy Day Fund. But the money from the hens went to Mama. To buy doodads with or maybe a soft new dress for when she and Pa would drive all the way to Council Hill to go to a dance with band music and singing. Now that it was autumn, all our fine feathered friends were going the last mile to market.

We had a double purpose in going to town: to get rid of the chickens and to register Bert in school. "You'll hate it," twelve year-old Myrna confided to him, leaning half over the front seat. "School is terrible. The teachers won't let you look out the window. Or scratch your poison ivy. Or anything." Bert's eyes got big and he glanced at a line of red blisters on his left arm.

Bob had to top Myrna. "Yeah, and they even got a special teacher who has nothing to do but snoop to catch kids playing hooky ..."

"Quit telling him that, " Ma interrupted. "You got nothing against school."

We groaned.

"It gets you away from the chickens, don't it?"

She had a point all right. Anything rather than chickens.

We pulled up to Van Vooren's Feed and Hardware. Just as we were about to unload, one of the kids accidentally unlatched the crate holding the Queen Buff Orphington — an amazing critter who ruled the roost with an iron claw. She let out an enraged cluck and her army began to flap their wings and stampede. In an instant, the car was filled with a snowfall of feathers.

Amid much noise and confusion, we managed to recapture Ma's clucking property and unload the whole kit-and-caboodle onto the scale outside the store. Ma marched into the office to bargain with the boss. We were still picking feathers out of our hair and ears when she came back.

It was kind of a tradition that Ma never told how much hen money there was. But the smile on her face more than made up for all the mornings that stupid Dumb Cluck had squawked me awake.

"What you gonna get, Ma?" Lucy blurted out The Big Question.

"This year I'm going to do something real special."

"What, Mama?" Everybody sat up and took notice. even Bob and Myrna quit Indian wrestling in the back seat. Ma never told in advance where hen money was headed. She'd say, "Oh, I think I'll save it for when President Eisenhower invites me to tea." Or, "Maybe your father and I will take off to Hawaii with the chicken money." But this time she sounded serious.

"What, Mama? " Bob prompted.

"This money is train fare," Ma said suddenly. "Come September, Vinnie is going to go to visit Aunt Lavinia for the school term."

"Mama!" I was nearly overcome. Memory stabbed me. Once Ma had caught me, my nose pressed up against the window, looking long at the sun going down behind the borrow-pit hills.

"What is it, Vinnie?" she said then, putting her hand on my back. "Wondering what the people are doing where the sun is still hot?" I shook my head. "Maybe you'll find out someday, Honey, " she had said — and I laughed because I know how things are with our family. We got a good farm — but we also got a lot of kids and hard work and no time for traipsing off to watch people or sunsets.

The car jerked forward as Ma continued. "Vinnie will go to school with Aunt Lavinia in Kansas City. And get a job. And ride on elevators and eat in fancy places."

"But, Ma," I finally found my tongue, "you know I can't go and do all those things. It's not right. It's not my money. I hated those chickens. Golly, last Fourth of July, I even fed old corn mash to Dumb Cluck so she would get drunk."

The back-seat kids laughed. Bob and Myrna had helped me with the mash. Ma didn't seem to hear.

"Lavinia said to send you — just to get you there — and she would find you a job and set you up fine in school. I want you to see a piece of the world before you marry and settle down and have your own family." Our old jalopy rounded Galena Street corner. "And don't argue with me now, or I'll remember what you did to my poor drunken chicken."

We came to a jerky stop in front of the school. "Thank you, Ma," I said in a small voice. Kansas City...Aunt Lavinia...movies...restaurants...the world! My heart raced.


The other kids took off to the playground while Ma and I went in to register Bert. Ma had used gooey stuff to slick his cowlick down and two or three tiny feathers were sticking to it. I defeathered him with one hand and straightened his shirt with the other. "Now, for heaven's sake, don't tell the man you hate school," I warned. "Myrna was only kidding,"

"Okey doke," he agreed. We went up the walk, Bert hanging tightly to my hand.

An official-looking blonde man whipped a yellow form out of the office desk drawer. He poised his pencil above it and fired questions in a very business-like way. "What is the child's name?"

Ma answered the third degree. "Albert Watkins--Rural Route 2--six years old--parents living--English at home-- never had diphtheria, small pox, typhoid, mumps, measles or insanity."

The questions stopped. The young man grinned at Bert. "Go sit over there, please." He pointed to a pint-sized chair and desk in the corner. "I have to give him an intelligence test to see if he can mange first grade." He ushered Ma and me into another room. "I'll call you when he's done."

The waiting room was large and modern, with flying saucer seats and big, big floor-length windows that opened onto the playground. We sat and watched the kids playing.

A crowd of them were gathered around a contraption called the Monkey Bars watching Bob swing from the bar by his heels and then flip to the ground and walk on his hands. "What a ham." I poked Ma. "Put him in front of a crowd and he'll do anything."

Just then, Bob lost his balance and landed in a tangled heap. The kids laughed. Bob picked himself up good-naturedly and twisted his legs around the bars again. I would really miss him and all the others when I went to Kansas City.

The door opened and the blonde teacher came into the waiting room. He chased Bert out to the playground. "I have good news for you, Mrs. Watkins." He turned to Ma when Bert was gone. "Your boy has an IQ of 140. Very high. As near to genius as I've seen since I've been teaching here."

"What does that mean?" Ma asked.

"It means that he is capable of doing schoolwork far beyond first grade level."

My mouth fell open. Through the big window I watched Bert climb aboard a swing. A genius? He looked like any other kid with freckles and no front teeth. I had thought that geniuses were pale little kids who begged to play the violin.

Ma seemed much less surprised. "I noticed Bert's real quick to catch on to things," she told the teacher. "He's been reading feed bags and comic books since he was three or four. And he learned to count by playing cribbage with his Pa and Uncles." She laughed. "The men like to play with him. They say he counts real good and he's the only one they know who don't cheat like blue blazes."

The teacher smiled. "We can help Bert a lot here at school. We have special classes in accelerated reading and writing and individual help for gifted children."

"That's wonderful," said Ma.

The young teacher lowered his eyes. "But to do it, the school has to hire a special teacher and buy extra textbooks and equipment. So...there's a tuition of a hundred dollars a semester for students in the program."

"Oh," Ma cleared her throat. I knew she was stalling for time, trying to think how we could juggle a hundred dollars from the budget. It might as well have been a thousand. There was no way.

Then, suddenly, I thought of the hen money -- my money. I tried to push the thought back inside my head. Ma's gift to me. My chance to see the world. But it was my brother's chance, too. I looked out the window. He was swinging with all his might on the playground swing. Faster and faster.

"Ma, " I said in a rush. "I know where we can get the tuition."

Ma looked hard at me, then down at her hands, red and rough from years of work. "No," she said. One firm, soft syllable. Then to the young man, "No, thank you, Mister. Just start him out in regular first grade."

We finished registering, rounded up the other kids, and started home in the old jalopy. Feathers covered everything and we were all worn out. "Did you see me go high on the swing?" Bert asked Ma.

"I sure did, Honey," she told him. "And just you wait. Someday you'll swing higher yet."

I thought we would turn up Talbot Road and go over the bridge through the quarry, but instead Ma took us another way. We zig-zagged along between fields of corn so tall that all I could see on either side were walls of green. Then, suddenly, our wheels crunched gravel and the road rose up, and on the horizon the Mississippi glinted like gold in the afternoon sun.

Bert was sleepy. He leaned his head against my shoulder and I put my arm around him. Ma took one hand off the steering wheel and squeezed my arm gently.

## Lydia Nowak

### Blood

your nights are etched in wormy
vanilla lines that transverse your face.
caught off-guard by the foot
of an angry barstool, one
eye looks in another direction

as you sit behind
the thick glass, inches but many
worlds away, in coveralls
that tinge your face and hair
a sickly beta-carotene,
my eyes feel for clues
to your mental state and
i realize what it means
to see the living dead

held back by transparent bars
like a wall of heat around fire
my fingers pick
at rough edges of cuticle
while you gnaw at stubs
of nail in the icy
stare of flat white that towers
over the short stools we crouch
upon, endlessly shifting in
struggle with protocol

and i know the blood between us
would file these walls
with toothpick to get you out,
carefully removing each granule
of stone in some strange ritual
of regression to the brother
i knew before so many ghosts
inhabited your eyes

**Constance Vogel**

Waiting Room: Children's Memorial Hospital

He flaps his bent-wing arms
as he chases children —
some bald, some bloated —
On the doorstep of adolescence
he is Gulliver
in a plastic play village.
His mother shushes his raw cries
that pierce the ears of those
who wait in their own chambers of fear.
Her tanned athletic body
makes him seem all the more grotesque.

The children scatter
as if he were a heron among sparrows,
scuttle into tiny doors
or run back to their families' laps.
They watch him dart, sometimes stumble,
down imaginary streets.
Grabbing for him, his mother winces
from elbow jabs and knee bumps,
wishes he were not the principal performer
but an ordinary face
in a crowd of extras.

## "Greetings from Quitman, Georgia"

I'll tool down I-65
past a blur of silos,
past Holiday Inns
with all-you-can-eat buffets, until
I reach an anonymous motel.
A geezer in plaid flannel shirt will unlock
one of twelve identical doors.

I'll toss my bag on the vinyl chair,
lie down on the green chenille spread
under a painting of a bullfighter
unfurling his cape of blood,
count sheep until sleep comes.

Next day at a u-name-it diner
a waitress with sugar candy hair
will serve unbuttered white toast
and in a Minnie Mouse voice ask,
"Where y'all from?"
I'll tell her Akron or Duluth
as she fills my heavy cup.

In a variety store I'll buy hair dye,
always wanted to go red,
maybe send a postcard to my husband--
magnolias blooming in a park.
No, he never liked
the way the petals rotted on the ground.
I'll keep going
till I reach Key West.
Maybe my car will sprout fins.

## Joni L. Biesemeier

### "There's No Place Like Home"
(excerpted from the novel *My Sex*)

If I could contain her image in a silver locket and leave it dangling around my neck, close to my heart, that is what I would do. Chew her up -- little spit balls -- attached with several pieces of hair that went prematurely gray. I worry that I too will be prematurely gray, that one day I'll look in the mirror and see my mother's image smiling, staring back at me -- a flat image that teases 3D -- I'll know that she is not only around my neck swinging lightly over my GAP wool sweater, but also rushing through me.

She's always hated for me to go, for something quite dangerous might happen. She points out that I'm helpless. She points her shriveled finger at me, "Your brother says you wore that purple dress again." The one that barely covers my ass. Suddenly I feel shellacked with shame; if something happens then maybe I deserve it. I give the mandatory hug and say good-bye until next year.

The road that winds between Chicago and Minneapolis and back again is flat. Cumbersome. If I've driven it round-trip once then I've done it fifty.

I tool down Highway 90. The family for two weeks -- too long -- inflated life's old anxieties and stresses. All this is the shame of losing job, losing face. Even the college grad can't pull herself together. I press the accelerator harder, glad to enter Illinois. (Not Minnesota. Once I hit the Minnesota border the speed limit decreased to 55, the roads turn to velvet and in less than an hour I exit. There's no place like home.) I reach over to open my purse, perched on the passenger seat next to me, and grab a Marlboro. The flame ignites in front of my face. Inhale deeply. Heart rate flares up. The whole premise of having a vacation...I had worried about asking my boss for time off. He solved that. He fired me.

I knew it was Christmas from all the rolled-up balls of red and green tinfoil and the cellophane wrappers camouflaged on the beige carpet. I knew it was Christmas from all the gifts strewn here and there, the favored ones taking primo places on the walls, on coffee tables, on the shelves, the unwanted ones lying dejectedly by the tree waiting for the week after Christmas when the tree would be dismantled. And the unwanted gifts would sit in the closet next to the no-shed fir. Save the boxes like a children's puzzle, the smaller one fitting inside the next larger size. Use these boxes next year.

Christmas. Families reuniting to watch the new ways they dance around each other -- would it be syncopated? To figure out if the gift is a metaphor or should it be taken at face value, much like the reckless gifts I pick out, scrambling, the week before Christmas.

My brother, buck-naked, lies in front of the Technicolor Christmas tree with large colored bulbs poised precariously on prickly pine. The evergreen scent lingers in the house. Jamie, slightly older than me, is just over a year old but his face is the same, as if only the naked body beneath him responds to time. Mommy sits, legs hugging her left side, painted lips match the mahogany stripes of her sweater. Stripes the exact width of the curls in her hair. Daddy before the dentures, his gap showing, he's smiling so large; a smile that out-glittered the tinsel on the tree. Ribbons and bows swirl around the contents of large boxes.

My body is shoved into a bright cherry red pajama suit with thin white stripes running at an angle across me. The fatted calf. The hood is pointed like Santa's, with a bell at the tip that jingles when aunts and uncles pick me up and coo. A flushed baby face resembling someone with a blood pressure problem swells out of the hood, two chins fat enough to connect. Did I quit believing in Santa then? How could I quit believing in someone I didn't know existed but was imitating? Someone played a mean trick on me.

That's what I hate about Christmas, all this trickery. On the twelve days before Christmas I lay in bed the entire morning -- the closer it gets to that magic date the more pangs ping inside of me. As the number of presents under the Christmas tree grows, insomnia festers and finally explodes full force. On Christmas Eve, with a stomach ache, watchful eyes identify shadows on the walls. I know Santa will never come if I don't go to sleep. But I can't sleep.

I left a glass of milk and three sugar cookies with red and green frosting in the shape of tiny reindeer out for him by the fireplace. I left a note telling him where the cookie jar is, if he wants more.

The last day of school before holiday vacation, I was at recess playing tether ball, whopping the ball back and forth to Jennie, when we heard this loud chop chop chop coming from the sky. It was a bright blue day. I covered my eyes with my hands to prevent the glaring sun from blinding me. I saw a shadowy movement — motionless in the sky — seeming to descend straight down.

Once out of the sun's direct sunlight a helicopter with Santa in the passenger's seat formed, the rays of sun pouring from all edges of the metal bird. Santa landed right in the middle of our grassy playground. The grass was green, thanks to the flooding we had earlier this year that forced everyone to evacuate the school early and take goldenrod school buses home, even though some of us lived only four short blocks away. This was a Minnesota winter but the air held the unusual promise of a pastel spring.

The pilot opened the glass globe side of the helicopter and Santa jumped out, spry for an old man. He stood beneath the chopper blades whipping circles above his head. He waved and began to amble towards us. Shy at first, I didn't want to be the first one over to him. I stalled, then bolted for him, my coat flying behind me.

Jennie, her overgrown bangs hanging in her eyes, yelled out, "Where yer reindeer?"

"Well, they're...er, they're at the North Pole resting for the big day," Santa chuckled and held his belly. He was wearing sheer, white gloves. Must be this spring weather. I looked closely at his beard and sure enough the elastic holding it to his face was visible. I'd been looking for the real Santa ever since I figured out there were a lot of impostors walking around: on street corners, ringing high-pitched bells, hoping the sound would squeeze change out of your pocket; in malls, sitting amidst pre-fabricated snow in glittery winter scenes waiting for me to come sit on their laps and have a Polaroid snapshot taken or a secret desire shared.

My secret desire was to find Rudolph's Santa, who would leave only red and green M&Ms in my stocking, instead of all those tan and brown ones that outnumber all the best colors. When I learned green ones make you horny and red ones make you grow boobs, I figured it was just as well Santa didn't ever leave only those colors.

This is the Christmas I purchased at K-Mart dish rags and a little statue of a red devil with a cleft chin and a triangle at the end of his tail. On the bottom of this knickknack it said, "I'm your horny little devil." Mommy can't stop laughing as she shows it to Daddy. The year before I got her one of a little angelic boy with doe eyes and arms stretched out. On the bottom of this statue it said, " I love you this much." She always displayed it prominently on the bar so I thought she would like another one.

I still go to Woolworth's and purchase knickknacks. This year it's snowing big tender flakes. Each flake a blueprint for imported lace. Fragile. Ephemeral. Each of the six points almost visible to the eye. They fall to the ground, melting in large, dirty, city puddles. Puddles of snowflakes. Stepping into the Woolworth's downtown immediately covers me with the silt of Christmas.

Lights — small red, yellow, blue and green ones — twinkle and gyrate and flash on and off, as if to captivate like an MTV video. Santa dolls talk if you press their cotton bellies, "Ho Ho Ho." There is canned snow for your windows with stencils of snowflakes; there are colored, potpourri-scented candles, tall and squat. There are beads, bows, and stockings hung in the aisles with care. I fight my way around people crammed into their winter coats, clutching red plastic shopping baskets filled with a little bit of this, a little bit of that. I turn a corner I hadn't noticed in the store and find a different entrance, new cashiers, new Christmas products.

A thin film protectively covers my eyes. Sensory overload.

In front of me are boxes and boxes of a variety of Christmas cards, half-price, 50% off. People aren't buying this year, the end of the first recession year. The scenes on the cards are of Norman Rockwell Christmases, animals with large eyes and human smiles across their lips. Inside the messages are gooey and fuzzy, only to be made more so by Mom with especially relevant words underlined once. Maybe twice.

Next to the cards are boxes of Santa suits. I look at the price — originally $35, now only $19.99. I pick up a box and eye its contents carefully. A thin, cheap angel hair product makes the beard, squared off at the bottom, perfectly fake. Flame retardent. Perfect for Jamie now that he's the man of the family.

The thin red synthetic jacket is lined in white, the pants turn out to be knickers with elastic sucking at the knees. Black plastic tubes put on before his black Reeboks pose as boots. A wide flimsy strip of this black vinyl wraps around his waist, plumped out with a pillow that keeps slipping down. He swings his stomach on his knees, carrying hideous not jolly fat in his torso. He is as simulated as the Santas I always encountered as a child but this time I know who he is. I dressed him.

I light another cigarette. Get my fill after two weeks of purity, denying to my ex-smoker mom that I now light up those Marlboros as frequently as she used to. Tonight I will inhale the smoke of two weeks worth of smokes. Tonight is New Year's Eve.

The good time ritual. A turning the channel from one year to the next, like a 1970s television, actually having to get up out of your La-Z-Boy to change the channel, adjust the antenna. Switch to snow. A loud, constant snow. What sort of frequency are the airwaves picking up? What, exactly, emits snow? On the television screen snow is loud and constant.

Here, outside the metal protection of the car, it is silent, blanketing everything in a calm, numb, methodical way. A hush. A hypnotic mesmerizer that slows you down and removes your head from your body. As I reach Chicago the traffic lullaby increases, singing me softly back into myself.


Sitting in front of a 1970s RCA Magnavox, you turned the dial. Click. Click. Click. Not too fast with the clicks, Dad said it's bad for the TV when you switch the channel too fast. You wouldn't want the frequencies to get confused. You still take a moment with each channel, drink in a moment of its picture or snow and proceed. There were only three channels and that was enough.

Today, with the remote, you flick through 54 channels and still have trouble finding something captivating. From one perfect picture to the next, skipping snow.


But not tonight. I squash out the cigarette. Tonight I'll arrive Chicago via Mpls and tonight I'll meet a man who I think is the man of my dreams and tonight I'll quit talking to my mother for two years and tonight....Everything changes on a dime tonight.

But, maybe not. I'm tired. I drag my blue vinyl suitcase up three flights of stairs and lurch into the apartment. The suitcase holds clean clothes and flimsy gifts. Unloading

presents is nothing substantial. Each year I set myself up for
the big let-down. Each year I spend more money than I
have, paying off charge bills until July, going into debt. Each
year I bring back another pair of pajamas for someone ten
years younger than me.

"What do you mean you don't wear these things
anymore? In high school you used to live in those." In high
school I used to live in sweaters made of cheap polyester
blends, obviously polyester blends, from a mother who still
recoils from wool and cotton.

"Why do you wear wool? It itches and you can't throw
it in the washer, it'll shrink."

Someone, everyone, seems to have stacks of Christmas
presents around them and I'm left with a few things that
don't mean special, that don't spell I love you, that don't
signal we were listening, that just sit there with a "blue light
special" aura. While I had groveled over a three-digit
sweater. While I ran last minute into Marshall Fields on
State Street, while I -- I too am selecting blue light specials,
gold-plated. Meaningless gestures that will place me in debt.

Once inside the apartment I look down the long, dark
hallway and see a glimpse of my roommates in the kitchen.
Rootgirl's pattern that of an isosceles triangle. The fridge,
the stove and the table, where cut vegetables lay scattered
around the chopping board. Lily is perched in the doorway
and leaning toward Rootgirl, chattering and laughing.
Having real jobs, their holiday trips home meant
abbreviated work weeks. Not the two-week sojourn I
thought would be good for me. A warm waft of soup greets
me and I linger, watch for a second in the hall.

Focus my eyes. The channel. A light frenetic snow is
blowing around outside. The inside of a store-bought
snowball shake-up scene. But not in here. In here there is a
clear picture.

**Paula Amann**

Graffiti

"Eros!", cries the spray paint--
not a challenge of the gangs
but lust on the loose
in the streets of Chicago.
Somewhere in the night
an unknown hand
scrawled it in white
across a shop window.
This is no battle cry,
just a bald assertion
of the body's right,
the heart's constitution,
a sign that even in
the concentrated grime
that marks the high-rises
and halls of state in this
sprawling, brawling city
by the lake, Liberty
runs clean and naked
in the night!

## Bonnie Tunick

On Sunday mornings,
Mommy makes us match.
And we get our cheeks pinched off
by people we don't know.
I always fuss in church
which makes my mommy mad.
My sister sits nice and quiet,
so I get scolded all alone.

Martha's gym teacher so strong and stern and very impressive. She can sink a basket halfcourt with a flick of her wrist, a defined bicep and frog thighs revealing years of dedicated weight training. Commanding respect with a warm smile and an attitude, the girls like to please her; to earn her praise for a good dribble, a nice setup; to secretly follow her Uptown where she shares a townhouse with another gym teacher with nice biceps and the same attitude.

Martha often breaks the rules so she will be held after class. The gym teacher makes her collect towels and sort pinnies and often lectures her on the value of teamwork. Martha never hears a word, dreamily gazing into her gym teacher's eyes. When they exchange big smiles, she knows they are kindred spirits. When Martha grows up, she will be a gym teacher. Or marry one.

## Jennie Kiffmeyer

### 2 lv.nts

### I.

Even though I left you
I still write you love notes.

This is one.

Nothing excited me more
than seeing
the jade Buddha of your necklace
against your chest,

brown from the Taiwanese sun,

sit
quietly
without blinking.

### II.

Even though I left you
I still write you love notes.

This is another.

When I see a woman walk down my
sidewalk
carrying a suitcase
or a brown paper sack
full of apricots

or nothing at all, simply

walking
past my kitchen window,
I wish she were you.

**Sara Tompson**

Geometry Defines a Closet

In public you are angular,
Thin, quick and all elbows.

Until we made love,
I missed your softness.

Even now in public
Your angles define you,
Keep others at bay.

If I move to comfort,
You accept my arms
But your elbows
Define their circle.

I acknowledge your tactic
As circumspect and wise,
But I miss your softness.

**Whitney Scott**

### Light Longing

Exquisite desire at our lips,
soaked with longing and sangria.
Hints of heat and sunrise;
warm hands know where to go.

Soaked with longing and sangria,
light flames our forms;
warm hands know where to go
explore with fervent fingers.

Light flames our forms,
Glowing, skin to skin,
explores with fervent fingers
an ache that's never needed names.

Glowing, skin to skin,
lips shine in shadow;
an ache that's never needed names
for sun-warmed fingers in the morning.

Lips shine in shadow;
strong, skilled hands trace designs
with sun-warmed fingers in the morning;
a laugh, straight from the groin.

Strong, skilled hands trace designs
with hints of heat and sunrise;
a laugh, straight from the groin;
exquisite desire at our lips.

## Joyce Goldenstern

### Wildcats

Jennifer was the oldest, then Polly, whom they nicknamed Polly Peapod, and then George. They lived in the country, an unincorporated area which later would become the tollway, the tollway oasis, and a huge shopping mall called Rosedale. But at that time there were just a few farms, a small country schoolhouse, and a few ranch houses built on large lots of land surrounded by acres of cornfields. They lived in one of these ranch houses — a $10,000 version of Frank Lloyd Wright with two immense picture windows in the living room: the front one facing Robert Road, the back one facing a picture postcard view of rolling land. Over the fireplace, their mother had plastered a huge panorama of a waterfall — no frame, no border of any type.

They had one dog — a beagle named Royal Roscoe and a series of cats, most of which were taffy-colored and named Taffy, but some of which were other colors and named Boots, Angel, or Jinx. But no matter what their official names, the family called all their cats "Kitty." The numerous Kitties all eventually, inevitably, ran away. Their father told the children that the cats grew wild because of the county fields surrounding them. Jenny, Polly, and George thought he meant like lions, tigers, jaguars — cats that would hiss, snarl, scratch, pounce on them from a hidden perch as they walked. Their hikes to the creek to catch salamanders were fraught with the dangerous excitement of safaris. They always returned to the ranch house before dark, but if caught out at dusk, Jenny could incite tears from her smaller brother and sister by merely sing-song singing a poem she had learned in fourth grade: "Tyger, Tyger burning bright in the forest of the night."

"Don't tease the little kids," her mother warned her once the screen door banged shut and they were all safe inside the ranch house.

Their father drove a company car and worked hard for the Lockport Utility Company. Often he would come home late, all worn out because the company had made him supervisor of a maintenance crew. Their mother was in charge of everything at home. She had one jar for each kid, each jar taped with their respective names. She put a dry bean in their jar if they did something right, like make their beds. She took a dry bean out of the jar if they did something irresponsible or disrespectful, like tie up the party line making prank phone calls.

Jennifer had the most beans. Polly felt jealous and hurt by her sister's natural goodness. Nevertheless, Polly continued to be forgetful and had to be reminded when it was her turn to feed Roscoe or dry the dishes — being reminded cost her a bean. George had the fewest beans, but, to use his expression of later years, he didn't give a flying doughnut hole about the beans.

Their mother got her ideas about raising children from *Family Circle*, the *Reader's Digest*, and from pamphlets displayed in a rack above the holy water fountain at the back of St. Vincent's. During the days of her dry bean experiment, Jennifer was ten, Polly was six, and George was five.

"Roscoe's gone again," George yelled one day. It would happen every once in a while. The children neglected to walk their dog because he was so undisciplined and enthusiastic and strong that he would end up taking them for runs through corn stubble and oozing mud. So he was tied up to a stake in the backyard where he would snooze all day in the shade of some bushes and eat twice a day the smelly red food they dumped in his crusty dish. But from time to time, the word "ESCAPE" spelled itself out in a cartoon balloon in his otherwise placid mind, and he would react with programmed alarm and determination, running repeatedly to the end of his chain, inching the stake from the ground with his stout neck, until he was free. He would take off down Robert Road with his long chain, and more often than not, the stake, in tow. The children would rouse their mother from her nap on the couch, and they would all pile into the Chevrolet to look for Royal Roscoe. If they couldn't find him, they would return to the ranch house to wait for a few days for the dog catcher to call, at which time they would pile back into the Chevrolet and go to the pound to rescue their dog. The children would marvel at how far he had reportedly gotten: Milfred Road, Prairieville, once all the way to Sandyhollow. Royal Roscoe would wag his tail with boundless good will when he saw them, lick all their faces, and pee on himself. "No hard feelings here," he seemed to be saying. They would bring him back home, tie him back up, and that would be that, at least, until next time.

The cats were more distressing. Gone for good, they would be. Though sometimes their quickly disappearing shadows would cast themselves on the front picture window at night when the drapes were drawn, or a dead rat would mysteriously appear on their front porch, or the sounds of a terrible squabble would reach them in the dead of night. Otherwise, gone.

George cried whenever they disappeared. Using the *Golden Book of Science,* Jennifer made up stories to comfort him. She turned to the picture of Carlsbad Caverns. "That's where they are," she would tell him. "Isn't it beautiful? If you look real close you can see a bit of Taffy's orange coat behind the stalagmite. They love it there. It's so beautiful."

"Is it like heaven?"

"Not exactly. Don't you remember from catechism class — cats have no souls. They can't go to heaven."

"I forgot," George mumbled, feeling ashamed of his mistake.

Polly the Peapod slept through their parents' arguments, her flat stomach pressed to the bottom trundle bed, smooth as a slice of bologna. But Jennifer listened to their accusations from the top bunk. When her father slammed the back door shut, she would pull the drape back from the bedroom window to watch him walk to the shed, clutching a whiskey bottle in his hand as though it were a weapon. The moon tangled itself in the branches of choke cherries and in the pumpkin vines in the garden. She imagined one of their lost cats perched on the window ledge of the shed, peering in on their father as he handled his beloved tools and silently drank whiskey until dawn when it would be time to get ready to go to work again. After awhile, she would crawl back to bed, and finally after an hour or so of listening to her mother's monotonous weeping, she would fall asleep.

Although Polly would sleep through the arguments, she was not completely untouched by the problems in the house. Sometimes at night, she would sleep walk. Jennifer would watch her, follow her into the bathroom. Polly would take the hair rollers from her hair and arrange them in neat rows in the vanity drawer. Jenny sat on the toilet and tried to talk to her, wake her with common sense. But Polly's body remained rigid and her irritated mumblings were non sequiturs.

One morning Jenny told her, "You walk in your sleep."

"I do not. Stop teasing or I'll tell Mom."

"I'll prove it to you." She brought her into the bathroom and showed her the neat rows of hair rollers.

"I don't, either. I took them out this morning." But Polly knew she hadn't. She felt scared. A demon inhabited her body.


At home Jenny told amazing stories to her brother George, helped her mother with weeding and housework, collected the most dry beans in her jar. But at school, her competency was not as noticeable. She was shy, afraid of the loud boys bussed in from far away — the kind of boys who could always find some terrible word to rhyme your name with. She wanted to make friends with June Kelly whom everyone ignored. She wanted to comfort her — as she comforted George — when the bully boys called her "smelly Kelly." But Jenny didn't have the courage to befriend her.

Jennifer stood alone on the edge of the playground watching rough Red Rover and Dodge Ball games, hoping only not to call attention to herself. One day Miss Weber said, "What are you dreaming about?" Her voice was not unkind, but Jennifer was mortified. She had been daydreaming about her fantasy family: six older brothers and a doting father who gave her a charm bracelet and a horse. She had been going over each of the charms on the bracelet in her mind. After that day, the boys began to sing "Beautiful Dreamer" whenever they walked by her in the cafeteria. She waited in terror for lunch and devised complicated ways to avoid them by being excused to go to the bathroom just before noon or volunteering to staple new bulletin boards during the lunch hour.


"Girls are easier to raise than boys," their mother said. When George took to lighting matches, she vowed she would punish him by burning his fingers if he did it again. He did. She did or tried to. She set him on the kitchen counter and dramatically lit a long wooden match. Jennifer couldn't watch. She knelt on the linoleum floor and wailed, sabotaging their mother's plan. "I'm not punishing you," their house-coated mother said. "You've done nothing wrong, so please stop crying." But Jennifer couldn't.


Two years passed. George brought Ds and Fs home on his report card and refused to do homework. He spent all evening sprawled in front of the television. Their mother gave up — "Girls are easier to raise than boys" — and took longer and longer naps.

Someone was digging up the field in back for a subdivision, so the children stopped going to the creek to catch salamanders.

George no longer cried when their cat ran away. He was developing a very bad temper. His bad temper centered in his neck which often turned a bright red and which had thickened to the stoutness of Royal Roscoe's. He and Polly were always fighting now — kicking, pulling each other's hair. Once George threw and broke a lamp. These altercations were each time more easily incited. Every word — "Georgie Porgie, puddin' and pie, kissed all the girls and made them cry" — every glance between them was taut with provocation.

One day George took a butcher knife from the kitchen drawer. "No, George, no!" yelled Polly. She ran toward the bathroom, the only room in the house with a lock. Jennifer screamed. "Don't kill her. Polly, don't die." George chased Polly with the knife with such determination that Jennifer was sure Polly would die if she did not make it to the bathroom in time. She heard the bathroom door shut and George pounding on it, and she knew Polly was safe.

She should have been relieved, but for some reason she began to cry and then to sob all in a heap on the living room floor. Her strange behavior made George and Polly forget their animosity. Soon they were standing together about three feet away from her, watching. "Maybe she got her period," Polly whispered. Finally their mother came, dressed in a housecoat, from her bedroom. "What is it?" she demanded, first with irritation, but finally with concern. "What is it?"

Jenny heard her question. The note of concern in her mother's voice made her pause, just for a second, to actually consider — What was it? But she did not know and not knowing made the sobs come stronger than before. As she gasped for breath, a vision flashed before her: her mother in her housecoat, George and Polly with their startled expressions, herself kneeling on the floor in the living room of the small ranch house, the house set in the middle of cornfields, and then the fields themselves stretching across the Midwest, seemingly peaceful, but in which all their runaway cats were hidden, just waiting to become tigers.

## Louise Schaefer

### 13-Year-Old Killed in Gang Shooting
### June 3, 1993

I thought the call would be an invitation
to visit the kids I'd left behind.
Brief niceties then
she wonders did I see the paper.
She asks do I remember Duy--
I thought she'd tell me you'd been
in a fight or suspended for
arguing with the sub again.
"He was shot last night."

I wait to hear, afraid to ask.
It hits me hard.
I feel my stomach muscles tighten like
a python around its prey.
I take a deep breath and then it comes.
"He died at 1:00 this afternoon."

I ask all the right questions:
   what happened?
   where was he?
   how are the other students taking it?
But I don't really care about the answers.

All that's going through my mind is
this seventh grade kid
who meekly tells me,
"But Ms. Schaefer, I don't know how
to write a paragraph."
Then we sit and talk and
the moment is yours.

"So it's like a car, huh? Ya got
the exhaust system and the ignition system

and if ya put a spark plug in the muffler
it ain't gonna work, right?"
*Yes, Duy, that's exactly it.*

I respect you and on this day
you respect me.
You say we are a team, me and you.
I am your pit crew.

"Duy's death brings to 24
the number of children under age 15
slain this year in the Chicago area."

To the Trib
you're just a number
and I'm surprised they refer to you as Duy.
To me you're the short Vietnamese boy
with the baggy-butt jeans who
fights with the sub when she puts you down,
the kid who made it to seventh grade
without learning how to write a sentence,
how to share a thought.
You're the boy who made me
believe I could really teach,
I could really make a difference.

Mary tells me your funeral is Sunday and
I commit myself to go.
But then I can't face you
in a casket.

On the other side of a desk, yes,
but not in a casket.
And so I choose not to face you at all
except on this page,
and at this time
         ...and every night in my dreams.

## Marie Micheletti

### You Have the Right to Remain Silent

She tried to ease the pain in her tired feet by shifting her weight from one weary leg to the other. Periodically she slipped off a shoe and rested a foot on the pavement. The warmth felt good at first, but soon the pavement was like a frying pan.

The sun beat down with the savagery of an a ancient god. Sweat slowly trickled down her body into her groin and started down her leg. The water fountains were broken, as usual. Even tepid water would have been welcome in this heat.

Her whole being ached for the cool of the shade trees that lined the wide ribbon of concrete, where the long rows of women moved slowly toward a low gray building. But she knew better than to step out of line for even a moment in the shade. She would never regain her place. In the past she had seen fights break out among exhausted women over lesser provocation than that.

When she stepped on the heels of the woman in front of her, she realized she was subconsciously trying to move the line along a little faster. "I'm sorry," she said, then moved back so quickly that she stepped on the toes of the woman behind her.

No one spoke. It was too hot, and the women didn't want to discuss why they were here. There were more young girls and older women than any other age in the lines, but all were between puberty and menopause. Remembering the irregularity of her early periods, she knew why the young girls were there. She supposed the same irregularity occurred to women during menopause. Ever since the Human Life Amendment specified that life begins at conception, any female whose menses were two weeks late had to register for the tests to determine if she were pregnant.

One young girl who looked no older than twelve was quietly sobbing. Others looked terrified. Since no sex education was allowed, they probably had no idea why they were even here. Some parents were along because they were held responsible for underage girls. The older women just plodded along with the resignation that comes from having been through this ordeal so may times.

Her own period had never been regular so she wasn't too worried. Despite that, a nagging fear at the back of her mind kept reminding her of the morning nausea she'd been having. They'd been as careful as they knew how but they didn't have much information. All the ways they knew, like using a vinegar sponge, were old wives' tales, whispered from person to person. All dependable birth control methods had been outlawed. Even the term "birth control" was taboo.

She should have been back at the office ten minutes ago. They would all know why she was late--no woman dared be late for any other reason. There would be men with their smirking faces and women with averted glances. The men would whisper behind her back and the women would keep a cool distance from her for a day or two. She didn't know why they always went through that stupid charade.

She had never yet seen an unmarried pregnant woman return to the office. But when a married woman returned pregnant, well, what a lot of fuss was made. All the clucking and fluttering over her. Like a bunch of hens! And the men strutted about with their chests puffed out like it was all their doing, patting her and telling her to take good care of herself and the "little one." As if she had any choice in the matter.

She knew from office talk that something people jokingly referred to as "M & M Rights" were read to pregnant wives and, from then on, all their rights, meager as they already were, were suspended. A State Guardian was appointed for the preborn child to make sure the woman complied with all the rules of pregnancy rules that controlled every part of her life, what she ate, what exercise she had, how much sleep she got--everything. Absolutely no medicines, except what the doctor ordered, not even an aspirin for a headache. No sexual relations during the last half of pregnancy. The woman wore an electronic bracelet to keep track of where she was, in case she went into labor. Tests were done monthly to determine if she had complied with the rules. Random checks to catch the careless or disobedient women were frequent. She'd heard one woman say that a Guardian had once come to her house, in the middle of the night, to check on her.

These were married women talking. Whatever would happen to someone like herself, who might be pregnant and not married? She'd never known anyone who was pregnant and single. Suddenly fear was grabbing at her throat, making it difficult to swallow.

Finally! She was past the registrar. The multitude of papers had been signed and now for the urine sample. A matron always watched to make sure it was *her* urine. That was embarrassing, doubly so, today. The heat caused her clothes to stick to her and she had sweat so much she had difficulty filling the flask. Done, at last. Now she could sit and rest her aching feet while she waited for the test results.

She wished she'd brought something to read. She'd already read the well-worn leaflets so many times she knew them by heart. Leaflets picturing plump-faced woman and chubby red-cheeked babies. They portrayed motherhood as the most joyous experience any woman could ever desire. But she had seen tired-looking women in the street, women with strings of children, like a comet's tail, trailing behind. Their faces bore no resemblance to these pictures.

The woman sitting next to her was called. Her face showed no emotion as she approached the shiny steel desk to hear the verdict. All married women were expected to look disappointed when they weren't "blessed" with the news that they were pregnant. She heard the clerk murmur her sympathy and the woman sigh and say, "Maybe next time," but as she turned away her face's brief moment of elation belied her words. Then, remembering where she was, the woman quickly wiped away her relief and glanced around to see if anyone had noticed.

She waited. Occasionally a woman would leave the steel desk and head for a rear exit. The huge gray door would close behind her with a thud.

Finally the clerk called her name. As she approached the desk, she sensed something different. Her throat became dry and her ears began to ring. Her heart seemed to enlarge until it filled her throat. The clerk motioned her toward the rear exit. She could feel eyes riveted to her back as she walked out. The heavy steel door shut behind her with the ominous portent of a prison gate.

An attendant handed her another flask. This had never happened before. Two matrons watched as she strained to produce the fluid. One gave her a cup of tepid water and, with that help and the sound of a running faucet, she produced the specimen.

She waited in a different room. The tension here was palpable. White-faced women stared straight ahead, not meeting each other's eyes. When they called her name her heart began pounding so hard she was sure that everyone could hear it. She went through another door, which led to a cubicle. She was told to remove her clothes and put on a shapeless gray and white striped gown. A matron took her watch, the pins from her hair, everything, including her purse.

With her heart beating in her ears, she could not hear. Her throat was so constricted she could not swallow. No longer did she feel the heat; she broke out in a cold sweat. Her hands were numb as she fumbled, trying to tie the strings on the gown. Everything seemed in slow motion. She felt as though she were struggling through deep water. Her legs were ready to buckle. The two matrons grasped her arms and propelled her through yet another door.

Her blurred eyes refused to focus. A black-clad figure, flanked by two scarlet ones, wavered in front of her. Faintly, over the pounding of her heart, she heard, as from a far distance, the droning of a chant--"found to be with child, and having no husband, and since it is inconceivable that anyone but our blessed lady, Mother Mary, would conceive immaculately, you have sinned against the Father, the Son, and the Holy Ghost. You must now be confined to such a place as will ensure the safety of the blessed fruit of thy womb. You have the right to remain silent--"

## Glenda Bailey-Mershon

Great Raw Woman:
(For my Grandmothers, caught between two worlds)

Earth-colored
great raw woman
riding hurricanes like a dream of fury
walking sodden land mired in muck
lifting rainbows from pastures
seeding bottomlands
and laying beds for oyster
soup steaming in the iron pot.

What you must have been in childbed,
birthing with the force of two hundred
hurricanes
crouching low, arching high
pushing out squalling life
and catching it in baskets
woven of blood and straw
in two fiery rough hands
rocking, rocking
face like the moon
over ravaged lands.

I see you each day,
squatting, rivulets of water flowing
out of your body across corn fields
over scorched meadows
And the red clay front yard
singing orange zinnias.

Your daughters are feathers
tossed by the same hurricane winds
brushed from your cheek
falling lightly
half a continent away.
Watching the moon rise in glowing glass,
spying your frame among junkyard shadows.
Strangers with tentative eyes
riding gently on fierce city rails.

Dreaming of lands where your bare feet fell,
feeling the earth beneath
a thousand tons of steel.
Even city towers gleam with your life:
skyscrapers like candles
in the hair of the Ancient One.

## The Spider and the Egg

Grandmother sat like an egg: Simple. Unadorned.
Self-contained.
But rough on the outside, as if the chicken
had swallowed too much gravel.

For forty years she sat. Years of widowhood, of living
as her children arranged.
Years of doing "not much:" a crocheted doily,
a tatted handkerchief,
a scrawled note to the brother in Washington.

Nothing escaped her attention:
The length of a skirt, the tongue stuck out
behind a parent's back.
Her daughters would hiss, and shun her country ways
while she continued to spin lace doilies
until every drawer, in every daughter's house,
was overflowing with them.

Her sharp remarks brought down quiet at the dinner table.
Crude speculation with sudden gusto
over who would produce the next grandbaby, or even
a change-of-life chick among her own brood.
Then she would follow up the indiscretion
by criticizing the potato salad.

Sharp-tongued as she was, she never argued.
"Whatever you say," she would croak, then
go back to spinning lace doilies
while you choked on your arguments.

She told stories reluctantly, as if
it were hard to let them go.
And if you pestered her too much

she would tell a different version
of one you knew well,
so you would give up on the truth.

Stories about her man, and about her mother:
How she hit him with a frying pan
one night when he came home drunk.
How her mother died from bad medicine,
while she (the egg)
stroked her saintly face unto its rest.

It was forty years before we all realized
her lasting spirit.
We all cried when she died
because we did not know we'd miss her so,
because even sitting is missed
after forty years.

Before she died she was too sick even to sit.
The nursing home aides had to turn her in her bed.
One night just before they rolled her away from me,
she lifted and turned her head and said distinctly,
"I love you."

With those three words
I felt she imagined me,
flung out her thread and caught me
in her ever-growing web.
Like a patient spider, letting nothing pass.
But needing nothing,
like an egg.

## Bonnie Tunick

Proper potty training is everything,
Edythe explained
as she finished ironing her underwear.

**Julie Sass**

Different Time Zones
(excerpted from the novel of the same name)

Wonder hopped out of the diesel but before she could shut the door, the driver leaned from the cab, handing her a crumpled-up bill. "Now don't go getting insulted, little lady. Maybe you can use some extree. I was glad for your company on this stretch."

"Oh, gosh...well, Samuel, that's really sweet of you." She stood waving until his rig was out of sight. Now who'd stop on this highway in Wyoming? Where was she going to spend the night? She reminded herself again that she wasn't afraid of hitchhiking. Really. Besides, there wasn't any other option. Dullas had cleaned out her cash before he left with Prophet and the other Flock of Believers.

A car was coming. Expensive model. She waved the Beamer down. As she ran toward it, she saw it had "MD" on the plates. "Hop in," he said, smiling, his eyes hidden by dark glasses. The back of her neck got that tingle and she hesitated. "It's okay. I've got office hours in Cody in forty minutes." She sat as close to the door as possible. He punched his radio, cranked it a bit. Natalie and Nat sang "Unforgettable" as he nonchalantly put his hand on her thigh.

"Hey, knock it off," she yelled. "I have a highly infectious virus that I contracted in Indonesia when I was in the Peace Corps. You can get it through clothing." She lowered her voice. "There is no known cure."

"Oh, really," he laughed, his eyes straight ahead. "Maybe I should examine you. Give you another opinion." He moved his hand up her leg.

She fumbled in her backpack. "I found this behind County General, next to one of those bright orange barrels." She showed him the hypodermic needle in her palm.

He screeched to the side of the road. "Out — get out. Are you crazy? I'll call the highway patrol if you don't get out." His hand was shaking as he reached for his phone.

She stood at the side of the road, her heart pounding. Thank the goddesses, Dullas had left a syringe behind when he decided thatt he could control his diabetes with vegetable juice as prescribed by the Prophet. She'd dumped everything from the medicine cabinet into her pack. But, of course, she knew it was no coincidence. Her spiritis were taking care of her, as usual.

A few minutes later, she stuck out her thumb. A semi screeched to the shoulder of the road and the passenger door opened. As Wonder hopped up, she met the sunbeaten, wrinkled face of a woman, sitting behind the wheel. "Get in here, young woman. Hitching on these Godforaken roads!" The driver started up immediately, stripping the gears and pulling onto the highway as cars honked and swerved to the other lane. "Where you off to?" She turned to Wonder, her blue eyes sparkling behind her glasses, the sternness of her mouth softening. "My name is Margaret, but everyone calls me 'Pearl'."

"Oh, no kidding? "Wonder smiled, breathing a little easier. "My name is Diana, but I call myself Wonder — like in Wonder Woman. And I'm off to New York."

"But, of course. The Amazon Princess. On the way to New York. Well, now, that's where I'm headed." She chuckled and pulled on the horn, startling Wonder and the driver of a pickup in the next lane. He gave them the finger and Pearl raised her spotted hand, making the sign of the cross.

Wonder settled back, rubbing the silver bangle at her wrist. What a blessing. A ride all the way to New York.


"You from around here?" Pearl asked.

"No, but I was born in Denver. And my great-grandmother, Pauline, my mother's grandmother, she's lived in Montana or Wyoming or the Dakotas all her life. She cooked for ranchers and railroad men, started when she was fouteen." Wonder's voice dropped. "Had to leave home — her father was mean to all of his children, but especially the girls. I got the feeling he was messing with her sexually." Wonder sighed. "Disgusting, isn't it? To think my great-great-grandfather was a child molester?"

"Disgusting?" Pearl thundered. "How about an abomination?"

"Oh, uh, right, " Wonder said, hesitantly. "I guess you're absolutely right."

Pearl nodded her head. "Go on now."

"Well, the story is, some cowboy...well, she was ...," Wonder hunched her shoulders, squeaking the word, "...raped."

The truck was chugging uphill and Pearl shifted, grinding the gears. "What? What did you say?" she bellowed. "Don't ever say that word softly, as though somehow she's shamed. Your great-grandmother was RAPED, RAVISHED, VIOLATED, INVADED." The sound filled the cabin, echoing in Wonder's ears.

"Wow, this stuff really gets to you, doesn't it? I mean for someone your age, like, don't you think you should calm down a bit? Can this be okay for your heart and blood pressure?"

Pearl shook her head. "W.W., there's nothing wrong with any of my organs or orifices. Women get into trouble when they don't let 'it' get to them."

"Well..." Wonder cleared her throat. "...Gram got pregnant from this OUTRAGE," Wonder yelled. "And no matter what she did she couldn't miscarry. She told me she rode horses, bounced down stairs, drank castor oil and gallons of Yarrow and St. John's Wort Tea and scalded herself in baths. Finally, she threw herself in Big Horn Lake. But two women from the Crow Nation rescued her, took her to the reservation and helped her through the birth.

She was really scared because her labor was so early and her belly so big. And then she had twins. Both girls. Twins run in our family. My sister, Frankie, in Chicago, has twins. But only one of Gram's lived, my grandmother, Angel. I always felt I was connected somehow to Native Americans because of that. One time, in Oregon — that's where I'm coming from —I used to live with this guy, Dullas --"

Pearl hooted, "Well, was he?"

"What, Native American? No, he --"

"No, was he a dull ass?"

Wonder said defensively, "Oh, he wasn't dull. I mean we had great times together. Exploring our former lives, learning to rechannel sexual energy into higher levels of consciousness, cooking to increase personal power, meditation, out-of-body — well, anyway, it wasn't ever dull."

Pearl interrupted. "Open the glove compartment, will you? Get me an Almond Joy and help yourself, too. I've got Hersheys and some of those chocolate-covered raisins."

"God, you eat stuff like that? Aren't you afraid of all that sugar and fat? I wouldn't put one of those close to my mouth. I've got some..." she fished into her baclpack..."trail mix." Try it, even my sisters will eat it. It's got nuts and sunflower seeds and oats."

Pearl extended her hand. "I know this concoction can't hurt me, but I don't get the point. You were telling me how you felt connected to a Native American heritage?"

"Well, I did, until Dullas and I attended a sweat lodge. We sat around a campfire under the full moon chanting with Theresa Wisdom Feather. I don't suppose you've heard of her?"

Pearl shook her head.

"Suddenly the most blood-curdling screams started and out of the bush jumped these women holding gourds filled with water which they dumped on the fire. 'You were warned, Patterson, you were warned,' one of them shouted, and old Wisdom Feather took off. Then they ripped down the tent that was the sweat lodge and started yelling at us.

'You have no right to trivialize our spirituality. You cannot become Indian. That is a racist act.' I expected Prophet to speak to them, explain how we didn't mean it, but he was gone, running alongside Wisdom Feather. So I got up and said I was really sorry and as I was talking one of them came close and looked at this glazed piece I wear." Wonder pulled the clay circle hanging from a leather thong away from her neck. I was scared to death, 'cause I thought one of them was going to rip it from me so I said, 'It was given to my great-grandmother by two Crow Women. You can't have it.'"

" 'I don't want what's yours,'one of them said, 'anymore than you should want what's mine. Find out what's spiritual in your own culture. Get the hell out of ours.'"

"I guess that's when I began to really look at what I was doing with Prophet. I mean, I had questions. Not that I was ready to give it all up, but when I began to ask about things, Prophet said I was allowing my ego to govern me. He prescribed all sorts of meditation and duties to help me get it under control, doing his laundry, cooking special dishes for him. But the night he suggested that I let him help me release the energy in one of my chakras, the kundalini, I knew it was over. I told Dullas I didn't want to be around Prophet anymore and that I wanted him to get out of his group, too. The next thing I knew Dullas and Prophet and the whole bunch disappeared. I came home from work and found my stuff gone, all my CDs, my laptop computer and the four hundred dollars I'd saved for us, working as an aide at the hospital."

"All the while Dullas was getting enlightened through meditation and learning at the feet of the Prophet, right?" Pearl rolled down her window and stuck out her fist with the candy wrapper, then looked at Wonder. "Okay, okay." She tossed it in the back. "W.W., you're lucky to be outta there. You wanta stop for some food? Like a hamburger, get your red blood cells stirred up? I don't eat much on a haul. Keep going with candy bars and a Coke. But I could eat a burger and fries if you want to."

"Oh, no. I don't think I'll ever eat meat again. I just think about all those chickens penned up, killed without ever having their feet touch the ground, cows gobbling up the grain that could feed the starving and pigs fattened until --"

"Oh, please. You're not going to wax sorrowful about pork, are you? Your kundalini would be in ecstasy if you sat before a plate of properly barbecued ribs. Mine always is," Pearl cackled. "We'll pick up Eighty in Nebraska, but I think we should gas up and take a break at this next stop. I don't suppose you've had a good shit since you've been loading up on pellets and grass."

Wonder laughed. "Pearl, don't you know that elimination is eased when you rid your diet of animal protein? You may be older than I am, but I think I can teach you a few things."

"But, of course. That's the whole point. So now, we'll each order what we want and maybe I'll have a bite of yours and you'll have a bite of mine. I bet your mouth is watering just thinking of a beef patty, steaming and leaking a little hot grease."

Wonder started to shake her head "no" but when she looked into Pearl's eyes, telling the truth seemed the only option. "Yes," she said, softly. Then shouted, " YES, IT MAKES MY MOUTH WATER."

*Japanese Woman with Snow.* Pen and ink stipple, copyright © 1994 by Anne H. Sheffield. Reprinted by permission.

## About the Authors and Artists

**Paula Amann** was born on the South Side of Chicago and migrated to the city as an adult. She still feels bonded to several Chicago 'hoods, but now makes her home among the treetops of Evanston. Her poetry has appeared in the anthologies *Wyrd Women–Word Women, Sister/Stranger: Lesbians Loving Across the Lines* and *Childless by Choice: A Feminist Anthology*. She is currently at work on a novel best described as a multi-cultural soap opera set in Chicago, with mostly women characters.

**Glenda Bailey-Mershon** was born and raised at the foot of the Great Smokies to a family whose ancestry has been mixed blood Cherokee/Catawba/European since the first Europeans crossed through the mountain passes. As a student at Knox College in Galesburg, Illinois, she first became accustomed to the peculiar flat horizons of the prairie. She has lived in the greater Chicago area for the past twenty years and has worked as an educator, an editor, a writer, and a political activist. Wild Dove Studio and Press, Inc. came about as part of her inquiry into the relationship between women and the environment. She has published several poems, some articles and technical writing, was the editor of the *Illinois NOW Times*, and is at work on her first novel, *Beverly*.

**Joni Biesemeier** has lived in many different northside Chicago abodes since 1988. She is obtaining her MA in English with a focus in Creative Writing and a concentration in Women's Studies at the University of Illinois at Chicago. The Women's Studies Concentration reaffirms her own writing and her own experiences. Cofounder of the performance group S-Curve, she is currently focusing on her novel, *My Sex*, which delves into the resonating factors between a mother-daughter and a woman/woman relationship. Joni works at a 9-5 office to pay the bills, and reads women's literature, works on her novel and does mountain biking in her spare time.

**Kathryn Brettinger**: I like to write about people, especially women, living on their land. My dad was an old-fashioned MD. in rural Indiana, and when I was a kid I rode with him on midnight house calls. The folks he doctored told him their troubles, of course, but also their dreams. I watched and listened. Once I helped deliver twins. I still live in Indiana, but the countryside my dad and I roamed has been swallowed by suburban sprawl. Exploring the still-beautiful area around Galena, Illinois, helps me remember.

**Andrea Cuchetto**, a lifelong Illinois resident, recently earned her BA. in English from Northern Illinois University. While she spent her youth (and is now living) in the suburbs of Chicago, she reveled in the time she lived further west where "there's more sky to see." Published previously only academically, Cuchetto writes from the perspective of a wommon with roots in radical-lesbian-feminist separatism, and has had more than a small portion of her outlook on the world shaped by the influence of a handful of 12-step programs and their supporters. She honored her sixth year of sobriety this past year. Currently employed in her dream job as a book seller, Cuchetto hopes to continue to craft her writing and to pursue graduate studies.

**C. L. Fitzgerald** is a recognized member of the Iroquois Confederacy. She has a BA in English from the University of Illinois. She was born in Illinois and has lived more than Illinois half her life there. She is a Native American activist as well as a poet. She writes about nature and our relationship with the earth, but her poems also have political messages. She has been published in several anthologies including some from The World of Poetry, as well as in college and university publications. She was a guest poet for Women in the Arts/Women at the Crossroads, a grant administered by the National Endowment for the Humanities and Radcliffe College.

**Carol Gloor** is a profoundly middle-aged lawyer and poet, trying to figure out what to do with the rest of her life. She writes only when she feels like it, and has published poetry in many small journals, most recently in *Korone* and *Metis*, and has a new book of poetry out, entitled *Before We Reach the Sky,* with three other women poets, published by One Potato Press.

**Joyce Goldenstern** was born in and has lived in Illinois most of her life, save for a few divergent twists and wrong turns. She lived for years in the midst of Northern Illinois cornfields, canned the stuff for several seasons at a Delmonte factory, but now resides in Chicago. Previous publication credits include *Quarterly West, Thirteenth Moon, The Little Magazine, Exquisite Corpse,* and the anthologies *Catholic Girls* (Penguin) and *In Her Own Country* (Third Side Press), among others. She is currently working on a collection of adult fairy tales and awaiting the publication of a children's nonfiction book about Albert Einstein (Fall '94, Enslow Publishers.)

**Mary Hanford** lives in Monmouth, Illinois, where she has taught English at Monmouth College since 1985. She was born in Washington, D.C., and brought up in Europe and the Southwest. As a Fulbright Scholar, Mary spent 1988-90 in Cameroon, West Africa. In 1995 she will return to direct the ACM Program in Zimbabwe, East Africa. Despite her travels, Mary considers Illinois her creative birthplace. Since moving to Illinois, she has been a featured poet in *Swamproot,* published a book of poetry, *Holding to the Light*, poems in journals, as well as short stories and articles. Mary Hanford credits Illinois' four seasons plus its heartland culture for her productivity.

**Stephanie Harris** is a native Chicagoan whose poems have appeared in various small press journals and anthologies, primarily in the Midwest. She is a member of and has served on the Board of Chicago's Feminist Writers Guild, participating in many Guild-sponsored workshops and readings. She performs her poetry in venues as diverse as bars, coffeehouses, bookstores, art galleries and the Chicago Public Library. Although she makes her home in Chicago, Stephanie's poetry has also been influenced by the childhood summers spent in Wisconsin and the four years she spent getting her undergraduate degree in Champaign-Urbana, Illinois. She is a vegetarian who loves animals, especially cats. On the lighter side, Stephanie enjoys collecting Barbie, and hopes that Mattel will someday issue a "Writer Barbie" for her collection.

**Wendy Heller:** I moved from Philadelphia to Chicago in my early twenties. I loved it from the very first, and did a lot of growing up and into myself in the arms of the Windy City. I am presently an Assistant Professor in clinical psychology at the University of Illinois in Champaign-Urbana where I do research on brain function and non-verbal experience (such as emotion, pain and the appreciation of art.) I have previously published poems in the University of Pennsylvania Press and in the Penn-Knox Press, and won a prize at the University of Chicago for the poem *Spartan Jar*.

**Judy Holman** lives and works in Evanston. She is a frequent visitor to Rest Cottage and is always humbled/inspired by the foresight, courage and stamina of Frances E. Willard. Judy is divorced and the mother of her grown son, Michael, who she describes as her good friend and best work. She works part-time at Northwestern University, leaving time to write her monthly article, The Crone's Corner, which appears in the Evanston NOW newsletter, *The Activist,* and in the *Illinois NOW Times.* She also facilitates a ten-week course on Feminist Thealogy, helps women create personal and public rituals to mark planned and unplanned passages in their lives, participates in the planning of a yearly Women's Conference, adds her energy to NOW and other groups, and always makes time to sit over coffee with friends.

**Clara Johnson** grew up on a farm in Macoupin County, Illinois. She is a retired chemist, a feminist, an editor, and author of *Suppressed HerStory, Johnson Stories,* and two unpublished novels. She is also Director of the DesPlaines/Park Ridge NOW Feminist Writers' Contest.

**Jennie Kiffmeyer** lives in Chicago. Her work has previously appeared in Hyphen Magazine, for which she is also an art editor. Currently she is a part-time student at the University of Chicago's Divinity School. Her favorite poets include John Donne, James Wright, and Federico Garcia Lorca. Her biggest influences are the Bible and Lake Michigan. She hopes one day to become Poet Laureate so she could spend a year traveling around the country in her car writing poems. Her favorite color is green. She dedicates 2 lv.nts to Irene Sosniak without whom she would be unaware of the potential for beauty.

**Marie Micheletti**:: I was raised on farms surrounding Camp Point, Illinois, close to Quincy. I actually attended those one-room country schools people tend to become so nostalgic about these days. I'll be 62 in February, born just exactly 200 years and two days after George Washington. I've been a registered nurse for forty years, and have worked in large and small hospitals around the country, ranging from university hospitals to city hospitals to one small Catholic hospital, until I married and settled in Tremont, a small farming community near Pekin, where I now work at the hospital. Reading has always been such a joy to me that I decided a few years back that I should really at least try to pay a bit of my debt by writing myself.

**Linda Mowry** lives in Mt. Prospect, Illinois and works at Prairie Moon, LTD., a feminist bookstore and woman-friendly space in Arlington Heights. She spends spare time in Northeast Indiana searching for weeds and wildflowers on land where her mother grew up and where she and her husband plan to retire.

**Lydia Nowak**: I am thirty-five and a life-long resident of Illinois. I have lived for the past six years in Plainfield, Illinois, but was born and raised in Chicago. I have a BA in Education from North Central College in Naperville and I teach at an inner-city Chicago elementary school. As a child, I never liked to read fiction or non-fiction books. One day, at the school library, I thumbed through a poetry book and became thoroughly fascinated by the rhythm and the emotion that was conveyed in such short space. I began reading poetry and tinkered with writing some poetry for special occasions. I rekindled this desire to write when I returned to college at the age of twenty-eight and enrolled in several writing courses. I have twelve poems published in the North Central College literary magazine "The Cardinal."

**Patricia Richmond** is a lifelong resident of the Midwest. She grew up in Detroit, then, at age 29, moved to Chicago, where she spends much of her spare time hanging out in coffee houses and bookstores. She is a member of the Feminist Writers' Guild and regularly participates in poetry workshops and readings in the Chicago area. *Horse 7/10* is her first published work.

**Julie Sass:** I was born and raised in Colorado, but moved to Illinois 33 years ago. So now I'm a native, I think. My writing reflects my background and my life experiences. I hope someone will read and enjoy what a white, middle-class feminist has to say, or at least not yawn in my face.

**Louise Schaefer** is a 24 year-old lesbian-feminist born in Waukegan, Illinois, in 1969. She grew up in Round Lake and moved to Chicago in 1989 to finish a BA in English. She is currently completing an MA in English Composition and is teaching composition at Northeastern Illinois University in Chicago. As an undergraduate, Louise was a student-teacher at Haugan Elementary School on the northwest side of Chicago. The poem *13 Year-Old Killed in Gang Shooting June 3 1993* was written in response to the death of one of her students.

**Whitney Scott,** a resident of the rural arts community of Crete, has had her writings published nationally in numerous literary publications including *Howling Dog, Amethyst, Kaleidoscope, Tomorrow Magazine, Letter eX* and others. She is a regular book reviewer for *Booklist.* Nominated for the 1993-94 Sidney Yates Arts Advocacy Award, Scott teaches writing at Chicago State University, Prairie State College and St. Xavier University. Her first novel, *Dancing to the End of the Shining Bar,* was recently published. Scott, who is from a family of European bookbinders, is also active in the field of Book Arts, and specializes in hand crafting one-of-a-kind books and marbled papers.

**Anne H. Sheffield** was born and raised in Utah but has lived in Illinois since 1967. She spent many years working for the Equal Rights Amendment in Illinois, first as Chair of the Peoria ERA Coalition, then as President of the Illinois National Organization for Women. Anne is a speech pathologist who now lives and works in the Northwest suburbs of Chicago. She likes to make her own classroom materials, including artwork like that included here.

**Evelyn E. Shockley:** I am a poet and short story writer, writing in the womanist tradition of Alice Walker and Zora Neale Hurston, for example. Through my work, I strive to envision what life could be while remaining grounded in what life is. I was raised in the South; however, I did my undergraduate studies in the Chicago area and it has been my heart-home ever since. Currently, I live in Bellwood, a near-west suburb of Chicago, with my husband, Terry, and my cat, Pasha. I write in front of the fireplace or at the desk in my second-floor "study" (*i.e.*, a small bedroom full of books.)

Ann Stotts received her masters degree in English and a women's studies certificate from the University of Illinois at Chicago in 1988. She has taught English at the University of Illinois at Chicago, Purdue University Calumet, and currently teaches at Shawnee College in southernmost Illinois. She has published poetry widely for the last five years or so in literary magazines nation-wide. This is her first appearance in an anthology. "Daughter Rite" was written under the creative influence of a film studies seminar led by Linda Williams.

Cinda Thompson: I was born in Marion, Williamson County, in Southern Illinois, grandchild to coal miners and politicians, and have lived in Peoria in Central Illinois for over ten years. Although I have traveled and lived elsewhere, the Midwest feels like home. I feel that, indeed, what "plays" here plays everywhere. If I had to make a statement concerning my work, I'd say I like to keep it simple. Most recently my short story, "Mayor Ben," won Honorable Mention in the national Des Plaines/ Park Ridge NOW Feminist Writers' Contest, and it was just published in *Downstate Story*. I have also given workshops and readings at area schools, libraries, museums, and bookstores. In previous years, I have published both poetry and short stories in numerous other anthologies — among them, *Women Writing About Exile* (Milkweed Editions, American Book Award, 1991) and *When I Am an Old Woman I Shall Wear Purple* (Papier Mache Press, American Booksellers Honors Award, 1991).

Sara Tompson: I am a 36-year-old feminist activist, environmental librarian, bisexual, and have been writing poems for two years. Like my farmer foremothers for generations, I was born and raised in Illinois — born in Oak Park, grew up in Glen Ellyn, Earlville, and Ottawa, obtained a BA from Northern Illinois University in DeKalb, and an MS from the University of Illinois. My husband and I live in Champaign. We have four fantastic nieces. "Geometry ..." was sparked when a close, strong friend was crying in a stressful public situation, then grew into its own self-contained observation, this poem.

Bonnie Tunick's vignettes and photographs are excerpts from her manuscript, *The Lines in Her Face*, a celebration of fictional women's life experiences and relationships, spanning a diversity of ages, backgrounds, circumstances and perspectives. Her poetry, photography and short stories have appeared or are forthcoming in a number of journals and magazines, including *Hyphen Magazine, Second Glance* and *Libido*. Bonnie is a lifetime Illinoisan, born and raised in Skokie, educated in Champaign-Urbana and Chicago, and currently residing in Evanston. She is just finishing her first novel and hopes, before turning completely gray, to leave her law practice to write full-time.

**Constance Vogel** was born in Wisconsin and is a resident of Glenview, Illinois. She graduated from Marquette University and Northeastern Illinois University. She has been an editor, high school English teacher, essay evaluator and sales associate. Her work has appeared in *The New York Times, Whetstone, Blue Unicorn, Willow Review, Hammers, Korone, Karamu,* and other poetry journals. Her poems have been broadcast on Dial-a-Poem, Chicago for four years. She has read her work in a variety of venues and won the M.U.S.E. contest in 1989, Mississippi Valley Poetry Contest (Illowa category) in 1992, the Ida Mary Williams competition in 1992, and has been nominated for a Pushcart Prize (1993.) Her book, *Caged Birds,* is forthcoming from Lakeshore Publishing.

**Cherie B. Weil** is a writer and illustrator who lives in Evanston, Illinois, in the house that her grandparents built. She attended Wellesley College and the University of Chicago, where she earned a degree in library science. After spending some time working with computers, she moved to printmaking and painting. Her print in this edition was done on Washington Island in Door County, Wisconsin, near a friend's house.

**Etta L. Worthington** develops and teaches management seminars. A single parent, she has lived in Illinois for nearly 20 years and now claims to be a Midwesterner, although she grew up in New York state. "Swimming" was written when her punctuation marks were on strike, and is an examination of middle age and motherhood. She has written three novels and has had poetry and short stories published in *Uruburos, Ariel, Spire, Radix, Arkenstone, Fan Magazine, Face to Face, and Wayside Quarterly.* She is also Editor and Publisher of *River Oak Review.*

Wild Dove Studio and Press, Inc. is eco-feminist in orientation and dedicated to providing an outlet for unpublished or little-published writers and artists.

We hope that you enjoyed *Jane's Stories* and that you will ask for other Wild Dove products at your local bookstore or giftstore.

If you want a listing of our other products, please send us the form below or write us at indicated address. We always like hearing from our readers.

— — — — — — — — — — — — — — — — — — — — — — — —

Wild Dove Studio and Press, Inc.
P.O. Box 789
Palatine, Illinois 60078-0789

Please send me information on other Wild Dove products. (Please fill out the form below).

Name _____   _____

Address_____   _____

City _____ State _____ Zip _____

Let us know what other products you would like to see:

_____

_____

_____

_____

FOL
APR 1 7 2024